How to Stubbornly Refuse to Make Yourself Miserable About Anything—Yes, Anything!

Revised Edition

Albert Ellis, Ph.D.

CITADEL PRESS
Kensington Publishing Corp.
www.kensingtonbooks.com

CITADEL PRESS BOOKS are published by

Kensington Publishing Corp.
119 West 40th Street
New York, NY 10018

All Kensington titles, imprints, and distributed lines are available at special quantity discounts for bulk purchases for sales promotions, premiums, fund-raising, educational, or institutional use. Special book excerpts or customized printings can also be created to fit specific needs. For details, write or phone the office of the Kensington sales manager: Kensington Publishing Corp., 119 West 40th Street, New York, NY 10018, attn: Sales Department; phone 1-800-221-2647.

CITADEL PRESS and the Citadel logo are Reg. U.S. Pat. & TM Off.

ISBN-13: 978-0-8065-3805-1
ISBN-10: 0-8065-3805-8

First hardcover printing: February 2006
First trade paperback printing: September 2016

10 9 8

Printed in the United States of America

Updated electronic edition: September 2016

ISBN-13: 978-0-8065-2653-8
ISBN-10: 0-8065-2653-5

Library of Congress Control Number: 2005934161

To Debbie Joffe, who helped tremendously with this revision.

Contents

Foreword

When I first picked up this book and read the title, I have to admit, I was somewhat skeptical. "How to Stubbornly Refuse to Make Yourself Miserable About Anything?—*Anything?*" That struck me as a very lofty idea. I can imagine that most people find this title intriguing, while at the same time find it dubious. "Anything" is a big word.

If you are able to get past this big word "anything" and follow Albert Ellis's recommendations, you'll find that this book is true to its title. Al, as he was known to colleagues and patients alike, proposes *musturbation* as the root of all emotional and behavioral disturbances. He encourages his readers to find and examine the "musts" that they are placing on themselves, on others, and on life conditions, for these are the basis of unhealthy negative emotions, such as anxiety, depression, anger, guilt, and shame, as well as self-defeating behaviors, such as procrastination, aggression, and addictions.

When Al began to develop Rational-Emotive Behavior Therapy (REBT) in the 1950s, he described a very important process that many individuals engage in, referred to as *secondary emotional disturbance* or *meta-disturbance*. Simply put, humans often have feelings about their feelings or feelings about their behaviors. It is not uncommon for those with anxiety to experience anxiety about anxiety; many people make themselves feel angry about their depression. This book applies the profound concept of secondary emotional disturbance to show readers the significance of accepting themselves with their primary emotional difficulties of anxiety, guilt, anger, depression, and so on—albeit, not *liking* the experience—rather than making themselves disturbed about their emotional and behavioral difficulties.

In addition to musturbating, we also tend to hold other self-sabotaging beliefs, such as *awfulizing, frustration intolerance,* and *global ratings of worth.* How many of us with anxiety find ourselves catastrophizing about what *might* or *could* happen? And what about those of us who are feeling depressed? Are we labeling ourselves "failures," "worthless," "inadequate"? Albert Ellis shows how individuals with frustration intolerance tend to give in to "short-range gain," with the result of "long-lived pain in the future."

Another helpful distinction Al makes in this book is that of emotional versus practical problems. Al very clearly points out that we all encounter practical problems in our lives (e.g., being unemployed, not in a relationship, etc.). However, as humans we have a tendency to make ourselves emotionally upset about our practical problems, creating two problems instead of one. Al makes the argument that in most cases it is important to address the emotional disturbance we are experiencing *about* our practical problems before we address the practical problem. Why? Recall a time in your life when you were in a very emotionally charged state, with anger, anxiety, or depression about something that had occurred or might occur. How successful were your attempts to come up with solutions to your practical problem when you were so emotionally upset?

How to Stubbornly Refuse to Make Yourself Miserable About Anything—Yes, Anything! is a must for your library. Each easy-to-read chapter concludes with an exercise for readers to apply to their particular life circumstances, making this book very personal. Al utilizes his extensive experience with thousands of clients to make his points on paper come to life. He also shows how he applied REBT to his own life to overcome severe public-speaking anxiety as well as social anxiety. For the first time, this new edition includes as appendixes the two pamphlets he refers to in the book: *How to Maintain and Enhance Your Rational Emotive Behavior Therapy Gains* and *Techniques for Disputing Irrational Beliefs (DIBS).*

Al's greatest wish and mission was to have as many people as possible learn and use REBT. Al was my mentor, and then I had the honor of working closely with him for years, so I am confident that he would be pleased to know that *How to Stubbornly Refuse to Make*

Yourself Miserable About Anything—Yes, Anything! has been re-launched in a new print edition as well as an e-book. Given that he wrote the majority of his books with his typewriter, I am sure Al would be amazed and gratified to hear that readers have access to many of his works in an e-format as well as print!

—Kristene A. Doyle, Ph.D., Sc.D.

Introduction: Bringing Rational Emotive Behavior Therapy Up to Date in the Twenty-First Century

I wrote the first edition of this book in 1987, when Rational Emotive Behavior Therapy (REBT) was a thriving forty-two-year-old psychotherapy. Almost everyone thought that my title was much too long—fourteen words—and that that would interfere with the book's sales. Well, they were wrong; *Stubbornly Refuse to Make Yourself Miserable* has been the most popular of all my books, along with *A Guide to Rational Living*.

Much has developed in the past eighteen years, however, and REBT has changed quite a bit since 1987. For one thing, since 1993 it is now called REBT instead of RET. Second, it is now, more than ever if possible, truly multimodal. It stresses not only many thinking, feeling, and behaving methods of therapy, but also (as I note in this revised edition) their integration and interrelation. So it is *more* cognitive-emotive-behavioral than ever.

Moreover, it is more philosophical—or more emphasizing philosophy than previously. Unlike most other Cognitive Behavioral Therapies (CBTs) it highlights three basic philosophies, which I have strongly espoused in several of my recent books, especially *Feeling Better, Getting Better, Staying Better; Overcoming Destructive Beliefs, Feelings, and Behaviors; Rational Emotive Behavioral Therapy—It Works for Me, It Can Work for You;* and *The Road to Tolerance: The Philosophy of Rational Emotive Behavior Therapy.* These philosophies follow from being aware of your dysfunctional and Irrational Beliefs, cognitively-emotionally-behaviorally Disputing them, and arriving at Effective New Philosophies or Rational Coping Philosophies.

The three basic Rational Coping Philosophies that REBT stresses are these:

Unconditional Self-Acceptance (USA) instead of Conditional Self-Esteem (CSE). You rate and evaluate your thoughts, feelings, and actions in relation to your main Goals of remaining alive and reasonably happy to see whether they aid these Goals. When they aid them, you rate that as "good" or "effective," and when they sabotage your Goals you rate that as "bad" or "ineffective." But you always—yes, always—accept and respect yourself, your personhood, your being, *whether or not* you perform well and *whether or not* other people approve of you and your behaviors.

Unconditional Other-Acceptance (UOA). You rate what other people think, feel, and do—in accordance with your own and general social standards—as "good" or "bad." But you never rate *them*, their *personhood*, their being. You accept and respect them—but *not* some of their traits and doings—just because, like you, they are alive and human. You have helpful *compassion* for all humans—and perhaps for all sentient creatures.

Unconditional Life-Acceptance (ULA). You rate the conditions of your life and your community as "good" or "bad"—in accordance with your and your community's moral Goals. But you never rate life itself or conditions themselves as "good" or "bad"; and, as Reinhold Niebuhr said, you try to change the dislikable conditions you can change, have the serenity to accept those you cannot change, and have the wisdom to know the difference.

REBT does not say that these three major philosophic acceptances will make you incredibly happy. They won't. You'll still have your and your social group's limitations. You'll still have the ability—the talent!—to needlessly upset yourself by making your healthy desires into *un*healthy demands. You'll still have physical problems to afflict you—such as floods, hurricanes, and disease. But your emotional-thinking-behaving problems will most probably be reduced—and so will your disturbed feelings about your thoughts, emotions, and actions.

What to do to cope with your own, other people's, and the

world's problems? Make yourself fully *aware* of your own needless tendencies to upset yourself with absolutistic shoulds, oughts, and musts in addition to your desires and preferences. See your own (and others') irrationalities as clearly as you can. Dispute them realistically, logically, and pragmatically. Dispute them thinkingly *and* emotionally *and* behaviorally—as shown in this book. Arrive at basic Rational Coping Philosophies, as noted above. Continue, continue, continue!

—Albert Ellis, Ph.D.
2006

Acknowledgments

I would like to acknowledge the collaboration of the many clients and workshop participants whose cases I anonymously mention in this book.

I also greatly appreciate the constructive criticism of Emmett Velten, Shawn Blau, and Kevin Everett FitzMaurice, who read and commented on the manuscript of this book but who are not responsible for any of its contents. Many thanks!

Finally, I would like to acknowledge Tim Runion, who did a fine word processing job.

1

Why Is This Book Different from Other Self-Help Books?

Hundreds of self-help books are published every year, and many of them are truly helpful to millions of readers. Why bother to write another? Why should I try to surpass my own and Robert A. Harper's *A New Guide to Rational Living*, which has already sold over two million copies, and try to supplement derivative books, such as *Your Erroneous Zones*, which have also had millions of readers? Why bother?

For several important reasons. Although Rational Emotive Behavior Therapy (REBT), which I originated in 1955, is now a major part of the psychological scene today, and although most modern therapists (yes, even psychoanalysts) include big chunks of it in their treatment plans, they often use it in a watered-down, wishy-washy way.

Aside from my professional writing, no book as yet gives a hard-headed, straight-from-the-horse's-mouth version of REBT; those few books that have attempted to do so are not written in simple, popular, self-help form. The present volume aims to make up for this omission.

More specifically, this book has the following goals—which I do not think you will find presented, all together, in any other book about acquiring mental health and happiness.

- It encourages you to have and to express strong feelings when something goes wrong with your life. But it clearly distinguishes between your feeling healthily and helpfully concerned, sorry, sad, frustrated, or annoyed and your feeling unhealthy and destructively panicked, depressed, enraged, and self-pitying.
- It shows you how to cope with difficult life situations and how to feel better when you are faced with them. But, more important—much more important—it demonstrates how you can *get better* as well as *feel better* when you needlessly "neuroticize" and plague yourself.
- It not only teaches you how you *can* control your emotional destiny and *can* stubbornly refuse to make yourself miserable over anything (yes, anything!), but it also specifically explains what you can *do* to use your potential for self-control.
- It rigorously stays with and promotes scientific thinking, reason, and reality, and it strictly avoids what many self-help books carelessly counsel today—huge amounts of mysticism and utopianism.
- It will help you achieve a profound philosophic change and a radically new outlook on life instead of a Pollyannaism "positive thinking" attitude that will only help you cope temporarily with difficulties and will often defeat you in the long run.
- It gives you many techniques for changing your personality, which are not backed merely by anecdotal or case-history "evidence," but which have now been proven to be effective by scores of objective, scientific experiments that were conducted with control groups.
- It efficiently shows you how you are *now* still creating your *present* emotional and behavioral problems, and it doesn't encourage you to waste endless time and energy foolishly trying to understand and explain your past history. It demonstrates how you *still* needlessly upset yourself and what you can do *today* to refuse to keep doing so.
- It encourages you to take full responsibility for your "upsetness" and for reducing it rather than copping out by blaming your par-

ents or social conditions for your going along with their silly teachings.

- This book presents the ABCs of REBT (and of other forms of cognitive and cognitive behavioral therapy) in a simple, understandable way, and it shows how stimuli or Activating Events (A) in your life do not mainly or directly cause your emotional consequences (C). Instead, your Belief System (B) largely upsets you, and you therefore have the ability to Dispute (D) your dysfunctional and irrational Beliefs (iBs) and to change them. It especially shows you many thinking, many emotive, and many behavioral methods of disputing and surrendering your irrational Beliefs (iBs) and thereby arriving at an Effective New Philosophy (E) of life.

- It shows you not only how to keep your present desires, wishes, preferences, goals, and values; but how to give up your grandiose, godlike demands and commands—those absolutistic and dogmatic shoulds, oughts, and musts that you add to desires and preferences and by which you needlessly disturb yourself.

- It informs you how to be independent and inner-directed and how to think for *yourself* rather than be gullible and suggestible, going along with what *others* think you should think.

- It gives you many practical, action-oriented exercises, which you can use to *work at* and *practice* REBT ways of rethinking and redoing your way of living.

- It shows you how to be rational in a highly irrational world—how to be as happy as *you* can be under some of the most difficult and "impossible" conditions. It insists that you can stubbornly refuse to make yourself miserable about some truly gruesome happenings—poverty, terrorism, sickness, war—and that you can, if you choose to do so, work more effectively to change some of the worst situations that confront you, and perhaps even the entire world.

- It will help you understand some of the main roots of mental disturbance—such as bigotry, intolerance, dogmatism, tyranny, and despotism—and to see how you can combat these roots of neurosis in yourself and in others.

- It presents a large variety of REBT methods for dealing with severe feelings of anxiety, depression, hostility, self-denigration, and self-pity. More than any other major school of therapy (except Arnold Lazarus's Multimodal Therapy), REBT is truly eclectic and multimodal. At the same time, it is selective and does its best to eliminate harmful and inefficient methods of psychotherapy.
- REBT is highly active-directive. It gets to the heart of human disturbance quickly and effectively, and presents self-help procedures that can be unusually effective in a short time.
- This book shows you how to be an honest hedonist and individualist—to be true to thine own self first—but at the same time live happily, successfully, and relatedly in a social group. It lets you keep and even sharpen your own special values, goals, and ideals while being a responsible citizen of your chosen community.
- It is simple and, I hope, exceptionally clear, but far from simplistic. Its wisdom, gleaned from many philosophers and psychologists, is practical and earthy—but nonetheless profound.
- It presents rules and methods derived from today's fastest-growing type of therapies—REBT (Rational Emotive Behavior Therapy) and CBT (Cognitive Behavioral Therapy)—which have grown enormously in recent years through their efficacy in helping millions of clients as well as thousands of therapists. It takes the best of the self-help techniques from which these therapies are formed and adapts them to the ability of the average reader to use them. That means Y-O-U.

Does this book, finally, uniquely tell you how to stubbornly refuse to make yourself miserable about anything—yes, anything? Really? Honestly? No nonsense about it? Yes, it actually does—if you will sincerely listen (L-I-S-T-E-N) and work (W-O-R-K) at receiving and using its message.

Will you listen? Will you work? Will you T-H-I-N-K, F-E-E-L, and A-C-T?

You definitely can. I hope you will!

2

Can You *Really* Refuse to Make Yourself Miserable About Anything?

This book has a strange message, that practically all human misery and serious emotional turmoil are quite unnecessary—not to mention unethical. You, unethical? When you make yourself severely anxious or depressed, you clearly are acting against *you* and are being unfair and unjust to *yourself*.

Your disturbance also badly affects your social group. It helps to upset your relatives and friends and, to some extent, your whole community. The expense of making yourself panicked, enraged, and self-pitying is enormous. In time and money lost. In needless effort spent. In uncalled-for mental anguish. In sabotaging others' happiness. In foolishly frittering away potential joy during the one life—yes, the *one* life—you'll probably ever have.

What a waste. How unnecessary!

But isn't emotional pain the human condition? Yes, it is. Hasn't it been with us since time immemorial? Yes, it has. Isn't it, then, inevitable as long as we are truly human, as long as we have the capacity to feel?

No, it isn't.

Let us not confuse painful feelings with emotional disturbance. Humans distinctly *feel*. Other animals feel, too, but not as delicately.

Dogs, for example, seem to feel what we may call love, sadness, fear, and pleasure. Not exactly as we do, but they definitely have feelings.

But how about awe? Romantic love? Poetic ardor? Creative passion? Scientific curiosity? Do dogs and chimpanzees have these feelings too?

I doubt it. Our subtle, romantic, creative feelings arise from complex thoughts and philosophies. As Epictetus and Marcus Aurelius, ancient stoic philosophers, pointed out, we humans mainly feel the way we think. No, not completely. But *mainly*.

That is the crucial message that Rational Emotive Behavior Therapy (REBT) has been making for over fifty years, after I adapted some of its principles from the ancients and from later thinkers—especially from Baruch Spinoza, Immanuel Kant, John Dewey, and Bertrand Russell. We *do* largely create our own feelings, and we do so by learning (from our parents and others) and by inventing (in our own heads) our own sane and foolish thoughts.

Create? Yes, we *create*. We consciously and unconsciously *choose* to think, to feel, and to act in certain self-helping and self-harming ways.

Not totally. Not all together. Not by a long shot! For we have great help, if you want to call it that, from both our heredity and our environment.

No, we are hardly born with specific thoughts, feelings, and behaviors. Nor does our environment directly *make us* act or feel. But our genes and our social upbringing give us strong tendencies to do (and enjoy) what we do. And although we usually go along with (or indulge in) these tendencies, we don't exactly *have to*. We definitely don't.

Not that we have unlimited choice or free will. Heck, no. We can't, no matter how hard we try, flap our hands and fly. We can't easily stop our various addictions to such substances as cigarettes, food, and alcohol, or to habits such as procrastination. We have one hell of a time changing any of our fixed habits. Alas, we do!

But we *can* choose to change ourselves remarkably. We *are* able to alter our strongest thoughts, feelings, and actions. Why? Because unlike dogs, monkeys, and cockroaches, we are human. As human beings, we are born with (and can escalate) a trait that other creatures rarely possess: the ability to think about our thinking. We are not only natural philosophers, we can philosophize about our philosophy, reason about our reasoning.

Which is damned lucky! And which gives us *some* degree of self-determination or free will. For if we were *just* one-level thinkers and could not *examine* our thinking, could not *weigh* our feelings, could not *review* our actions, where would we be? Pretty well stuck!

Actually, we are not stuck or habit-bound—if we *choose* not to be. For we can be aware of our surroundings and also aware of *ourselves*. We are born—yes, born—with a rare potential for observing and thinking about our *own* behavior. Not that other animals (primates, for example) have *no* self-consciousness. They do have *some*. But not much.

We humans have real self-awareness. We *can*, though we do not *have to*, observe and judge our own goals, desires, and purposes. We *can* examine, review, and change them. We can also see and reflect upon our *changed* ideas, emotions, and doings. And we can change *them*. And change them again—and again!

Now let's not run this idea of "self-change" into the ground. Of course we *have* this capacity. Of course we *can* use it, but not without limits—not perfectly. We get our original goals and desires largely from our biological tendencies and from our early childhood training.

We *like* mother's milk (or bottled formulas), and we *enjoy* nestling up to our parents' bodies. We like mother's milk and parental cuddling because we are *born* to like them, are *trained* to like them, and become *habituated* to liking them. So what we call our desires and preferences are not all *freely* chosen. Many are instilled in us by our heredity and our conditioning.

The more we choose to *use* our self-awareness and to *think* about our goals and desires, the more we create—yes, create—free will or self-determination. That also goes for our emotions, both our healthy and our disturbed feelings. Take, for instance, your own feelings of frustration and disappointment when you suffer a loss. Someone promises to give you a job, for example, or to lend you some money, and then backs down. Naturally, you feel annoyed and sad. Good. Those negative feelings acknowledge that you are not getting what you want and encourage you to look for another job or another loan.

So, your feelings of annoyance and sadness are at first uncomfortable and "bad." In the long run, however, they tend to help you get more of what you want and less of what you don't want.

Do you have a choice of these healthy negative feelings when something goes wrong in your life? Yes. You may choose to feel *very* annoyed—or a little annoyed. You may choose to focus on the advantages of losing a promised job (such as the opportunity to try for a better one) and hardly feel annoyed at all. Or you may choose to put down the person who falsely promised you the job and feel happy about being a "better person" than this "louse."

You may also choose to highlight the disadvantages of getting the promised job (for example, the hassle of commuting to work) and actually make yourself feel quite pleased about not getting it. You might have to work at not feeling sad and annoyed about losing the job, but you could definitely *choose* to do so.

So you do have a choice about your *natural* or *normal* reactions to losing a job (or a loan or anything else). Usually, you would not bother to exert this choice, and you would choose to accept the normal, healthy feelings of annoyance and disappointment, using them in the future to help you. You would live with them and benefit from them.

Now let us suppose that when you are unfairly deprived of a job or a loan you make yourself feel severely anxious, depressed, self-denigrated, or enraged. You see that you are being treated unfairly. You upset yourself immensely about their unfairness.

Can you still choose to have or not have *these* strong, off-the-wall feelings?

Definitely, yes. Clearly, you can.

That is the main theme of this book: No matter how badly you act, no matter how unfairly others treat you, no matter how crummy are the conditions you live under—you virtually always (*yes*, A-L-W-A-Y-S) have the ability and the power to change your intense feelings of anxiety, despair, and hostility. Not only can you decrease them, you can practically annihilate and remove them. *If you use the methods outlined in the following chapters. If you work at using them!*

When you suffer a real loss, are your feelings of panic, depression, and rage unnatural? No, they are so natural, so normal that they are a basic part of the human condition. They are exceptionally common and universal. Virtually all of us have them—and often! It would be most strange if you did not feel them fairly frequently.

But *normal* or *common* doesn't mean *healthy*. Colds are very common. So are bruises, broken bones, and infections. But they are hardly good or beneficial!

So it is with feelings of anxiety. Concern, caution, vigilance, and what we may call light anxiety are normal and *healthy*. If you had absolutely zero anxiety you would fail to watch where you're going or how you're doing, and you would soon get into trouble and perhaps even kill yourself.

But severe anxiety, nervousness, dread, and panic are normal (or frequent) but *un*healthy. Severity of anxiety leads to dismal *over*concern, to terror, and to horror. It can freeze you and help you to behave incompetently and unsocially. So by all means, keep your feelings of concern and caution but junk your feelings of overconcern, "awfulizing," panic, and dread.

How? First, acknowledge that the two feelings are quite different, and don't quibble or rationalize that anxiety is a healthy condition. Don't claim that anxiety is inevitable and has to be accepted as long as you live. No. Concern or caution is almost inevitable (and good) for you. But not panic and horror.

What is the difference between concern and panic?

The difference stems from seeing the things you desire as *absolute necessities*. As I pointed out in *A Guide to Rational Living*, you create severe anxiety when you jump from inclination to "*must*urbation."

If you *prefer* to perform well and *want* to be accepted by others, you are *concerned* that you will fail and be rejected. Your healthy concern encourages you to act competently and nicely. But if you devoutly believe that you absolutely, under all conditions, *must* perform well and that you *have to* be accepted by others, you will then tend to make yourself—yes, *make* yourself—panicked if you don't perform as well as you supposedly *must*.

What luck! If the theories of Epictetus, Karen Horney (who first talked about the "tyranny of the shoulds"), Alfred Korzybski (the founder of general semantics), and REBT are correct, you almost always bring on your emotional problems by rigidly adopting one of the basic methods of crooked thinking—*must*urbation. Therefore, if you understand how you upset yourself by slipping into irrational shoulds, oughts, demands, and commands, unconsciously sneaking them into your thinking, you can just about always stop disturbing yourself about anything.

Always? No, *just about* always.

For there are, as discussed later, a few exceptions to the rule of *must*urbation. But in about ninety-five out of a hundred cases, you can spot your *must*urbatory thinking, feeling, and behaving; change them; and refuse to be miserable about the hassles that you "normally" upset yourself about.

Really? Yes, really, as you can rationally figure out if you *think* about it.

Can I prove this REBT claim? I think that I can. Modern psychology has done many experiments showing that panicked and depressed people have been able, by changing their outlooks, to overcome their disturbed feelings and to lead much happier lives. Recently, thanks to researchers who do studies of Rational Emotive Behavior Therapy, Cognitive Therapy, and other Cognitive Behavioral Therapies, more than two hundred controlled scientific studies have shown that teaching people how to change some of their negative ideas helps them to feel and act much better. Hundreds of other studies indicate that the main techniques used in REBT work effectively.

Still another batch of scientific studies—at the present writing, over 250 of them—have tested whether the main irrational Beliefs (iBs) that people hold (and that I pointed out in 1956) actually show how emotionally disturbed they are. About 95 percent of these studies show that people who have serious emotional problems admit that they have more irrational beliefs than people who have lesser problems.

Does all this scientific evidence prove that you can easily discover your unconditional, rigid shoulds, oughts, musts, commands, and demands that make you miserable and soon give them up? Can you quickly become a clear thinker and thereafter lead a carefree life?

Not necessarily! It takes, as the rest of this book will show, more than that. But there is an answer. You definitely can see, dispute, and surrender the irrational ideas with which you upset yourself. You can use scientific thinking to uproot your self-defeating dogmas.

How? Read the next chapter and see.

But first, an exercise.

REBT Exercise No. 1

At first, the following exercise seems very simple, but it is not quite as easy as it appears. It gives you practice at distinguishing between your *healthy* and your *unhealthy* negative feelings when you view something in your life as "unfortunate" or when you are concerned about a "bad" event occurring.

DISTINGUISHING BETWEEN HEALTHY CONCERN, CAUTION, VIGILANCE, AND UNHEALTHY ANXIETY, NERVOUSNESS, AND PANIC

Imagine an unfortunate thing that might happen to you soon, such as losing a good job, being hurt in an accident, or losing a loved one. Vividly imagine that this event may easily occur. How do you feel? What are you telling yourself in order to create this feeling?

If you feel *healthy* concern or caution, you are telling yourself something such as, "I certainly wouldn't like this unfortunate thing to happen, but if it does occur, I can handle it." "If my mate were very ill or dead, that would be very sad, but I could still live and be reasonably happy." "If I lost my sight, that would be exceptionally handicapping, but I could still have a good many enjoyments."

Notice that all these thoughts state how deprived and sorry you would be if certain events occurred, but all add a *but* that would still leave you an option for living and enjoying life.

If you feel unhealthy anxiety, nervousness, or panic, look for these kinds of *musts, necessities, awfulizings, I-can't-stand-its, self-downings,* and *overgeneralizations:* "If I lost my job, as I *must* not, I could *never* get a good one again, and that would show what a wholly *incompetent person* I am!" "I must have a *guarantee* that my mate *must* not die, for if he or she did, I *couldn't stand* being alone and would *always* be miserable." "It's *absolutely necessary* that I not lose my sight, for if I did, my life would be *awful* and *horrible*, and I could never enjoy anything again!"

Note that these are predictions of unconditional and complete pain and that they leave you *no* way out of continual suffering.

Imagine, again, that something dreadful has actually happened to you, such as losing all your money, having a boss who is always criticizing you, or being treated unfairly by your best friend or mate. Do you, as you imagine this, feel *only* sorry, sad, and regretful? Or do you *also* feel unhealthily depressed or angry?

If you feel depressed, look for *shoulds, oughts,* and *musts* like these: "I *should* have been more careful with my money. What a fool I was for not being more cautious!" "My boss *ought* not criticize me like that! I *can't bear* that kind of continual criticism!"

If you feel very angry, look for *must*urbating self-statements like these: "My best friend *must* not treat me that unfairly! What a thorough louse he is!" "My living conditions *have* to be better than they are! How unjust and horrible it is that things are this way!"

Whenever you have strong negative feelings because unfortunate things are actually happening to you or you imagine that they might occur, see whether these feelings healthfully follow from your *wishes* and *desires* to have better things occur. Or are you creating them by going beyond your preferences and inventing powerful *shoulds, oughts, musts, demands, commands,* and *necessities*? If so, you are turning concern and caution into *over*concern, severe anxiety, and panic. Observe the real difference in your feelings!

3

Can Scientific Thinking Remove Your Emotional Misery?

You can figure out by sheer logic that if you were only—and I mean *only*—to stay with your desires and preferences, and if you were never—and I mean *never*—to stray into unrealistic demands that your desires *have to* be fulfilled, you could very rarely disturb, *really* disturb, yourself about anything. Why?

Because your preferences start off with, "I would very much *like* or *prefer* to have success, approval, or comfort," and then end with the conclusion, "*But* I don't *have* to have it. I won't die without it. And I could be happy (though not *as* happy) without it."

Or your preferences begin with, "I would distinctly *dislike* or *abhor* failure, rejection, or pain, but I *can stand it*. I won't *collapse*. I can *still* be reasonably happy (though not *as* happy) if I have these unfortunate experiences."

When you insist, however, that you always *must* have or do something, you often think in this way: "Because I would very much *like* or *prefer* to have success, approval, or pleasure, I absolutely, under practically all conditions, *must* have it. And if I don't get it, as I completely *must*, it's *awful*, I *can't stand it*, I am an *inferior person* for not arranging to get it, and the world is a *horrible place* for not giving me what I *must* have! I am sure that I'll *never* get it, and therefore I can't be happy *at all*!"

When you think in this rigid, *mus*turbatory way, you will frequently feel anxious, depressed, self-hating, hostile, and self-pitying. Just stick to your profound, rigid *shoulds, oughts,* and *musts,* and you will see how you *feel*!

Are dogmatic and unconditional *musts* the only causes of emotional problems? No, not exactly. Some disturbances, such as psychosis and epilepsy, may include few *musts*. Other mental problems, such as severe depression and alcoholism, may involve physical ailments that actually create, as well as are created by, musts and other forms of crooked thinking.

But the usual kinds of emotional disturbances or neuroses (such as most feelings of anxiety and rage) largely come from grandiose thinking. Even when you have great feelings of inadequacy? Yes, your inferiority feelings are, ironically, the result of your godlike demands.

Take Stevie, for example. Twenty-three, with a law degree and well on his way to becoming a CPA, Stevie seemed to have everything anyone could want. Including a great build, almost perfect features, and adoring—and filthy rich—parents. Yet, Stevie was a social basket case—with no friends, no dates, unable to talk about anything but law and business. And he thoroughly hated himself.

Did Stevie have an older brother who was much better at socializing?

Was he unconsciously guilty about lusting after his mother?

Had he struck out on the ball field with three kids on base and been laughed at by all his sixth-grade classmates?

Did his father yell at him for masturbating and threaten to cut his penis off?

None of the above. Stevie had few childhood traumas and succeeded at almost everything he did. But . . . ?

By the time he reached puberty, in spite of the love and acceptance of his parents, and in spite of his fine performance at school and at sports, Stevie hated himself. Why?

Because he was lousy at conversation. He had a high-pitched voice and a slight lisp. And, perfectionist that he was, he demanded of himself that he speak beautifully. But the more he insisted that he had to speak very well, the more he stuttered and stammered. Then he mainly shut up and withdrew.

By the time he was twenty-three, everyone knew Stevie as an exceptionally shy, inhibited young man. No one doubted his self-hatred. But few realized his underlying grandiosity—his absolute need to be perfect and ideal in every respect and his complete refusal to accept any kind of mediocrity. Only after several months of REBT was I able to show Stevie that he was laying many *shoulds* on himself. Such as: "I have to be great at *every* important thing. And when I talk stupidly or badly *at all*, as I absolutely *must not*, I am completely worthless. So why, when I cannot speak outstandingly well, try at all?"

At first, Stevie couldn't admit his perfectionism. But he finally saw his godlike demands on himself. Once he recognized these demands and began to use REBT to dispute them, and once he began to feel that he didn't *have to* speak beautifully, he lost his feelings of inadequacy. Even though he still lisped and talked in a high-pitched voice, he stopped withdrawing and forced himself to keep talking and talking—and finally became a good conversationalist.

Not all emotional disturbance stems from arrogant thinking. But much of it does. And when you demand that you *must* not have failings, you can also demand that you must not be neurotic. Stevie, for example, clearly saw that he was neurotic—and then put himself down for being disturbed and hence made himself *more* neurotic.

Thus, he told himself, "Other people aren't as shy as I am. How nutty of me to be so shy when most others don't have this problem. I must not be!" "How stupid of me to be this disturbed!" So I created a secondary problem—a neurosis about my neurosis!

When you are neurotic, you frequently make yourself that way with illogical and unrealistic thinking. First, you are born with a talent for accepting and creating self-damaging ideas. Then you are considerably aided by your environment—which gives you real troubles (such as poverty, disease, and injustice) and which often encourages your rigid thinking (such as, "Since you have musical ability, you absolutely *ought* to be an outstanding musician.").

But neurosis still comes mainly from *you*. You consciously or unconsciously *choose* to victimize yourself by it. And you *can* choose to stop your nonsense and to stubbornly refuse to make yourself neurotic about virtually anything.

You really *can*?

Yes, that is the main thrust of this book. You can think scientifically. As the brilliant psychologist George Kelly pointed out in 1955, you are a natural scientist. Thus, you *predict* what will happen if you decide to save money and buy a good car. And, once you decide, you *observe* the results of your decision and *check* them to try to *confirm* your predictions. Will you actually be able to save enough? Will you, if you do not, get a good car? You check to see.

That is the essence of science: setting up plausible hypotheses or guesses and then experimenting and checking to uphold or disprove them. For a hypothesis is not a *fact*—only a guess, an assumption. And you check it to determine if it is correct. If it proves false, you reject it and try a new hypothesis. If it seems correct, you tentatively keep it—but always stand ready to change it if later evidence against it arises.

This is the scientific method. It is hardly infallible and often produces uncertain results. But it is probably the best method we have of discovering "truth" and of understanding "reality." Many mystics and religionists have argued that science gives us only a *limited* view of reality and that we can achieve Absolute Truth and Cosmic Understanding by pure intuition or direct experiences of the central energy of the universe. Interesting theories—or hypotheses! But hardly as yet proved. And most likely we can never prove or disprove them. Therefore, they are not science.

Science is not merely the use of logic and facts to verify or falsify a theory. More important, it consists of continually revising and changing theories and trying to replace them with more valid ideas and more useful guesses. It is flexible rather than rigid, open-minded instead of dogmatic. It strives for a greater truth but not for absolute and perfect truth (with a capital T!).

The principles of REBT outlined in this book uniquely hold that anti-scientific, irrational thinking is a main cause of emotional disturbance and that if REBT persuades you to be an efficient scientist, you will know how to stubbornly refuse to make yourself miserable about practically anything. Yes, anything!

For if you are consistently scientific and flexible about your desires, preferences, and values, you will not escalate them into self-defeating dogmas. You will then think, "I strongly prefer to have a fine career and be with a partner I love." But you will not fanatically—and unscientifically!—add: (a) "I *must* have a fine career!" (b) "I can *only* be happy with a partner I love!" (c) "I am a *thoroughly rotten person* if I don't achieve the fine career and great relationship I *must* achieve!"

REBT also shows you that if you do, somehow, devoutly believe these rigid *musts* and thereby make yourself miserable, you can always use the scientific method to dispute and uproot them, then begin thinking sanely again. For that is what emotional health largely is—sane or scientific thinking. It is next to impossible, REBT holds, to make and keep yourself seriously neurotic if you give up all dogma, all bigotry, all intolerance. For if you think scientifically, you can *accept*—though hardly *like*—unchangeable hassles and stop making them into "holy horrors."

Of course, you always *won't* do this. In no way!

You have as much chance to be a perfect scientist as you have, say, to be a perfect pianist or writer. As a very *fallible* human being, you'll hardly reach perfection!

You can strive, if you wish, to be *as* good as you can be. But you'd better not try for perfection! You can *wish* for it, *prefer* to achieve it, and thereby refuse to upset yourself if you fall short. Even *desiring* real perfection seems futile. But to *demand* it seems—well, almost perfectly insane! Or, as Alfred Korzybski put it, unsane.

So even if you thoroughly read this book and energetically strive to follow its suggestions, you will not become a perfect scientist—or make yourself completely "unmiserable" for the rest of your life. To reap this kind of utopian harvest, try some devout cult that promises pure bliss forever. Science will not. But here is a more realistic REBT plan:

To challenge your misery, try science. Give it a real chance. Work at thinking rationally, sticking to reality, checking your hypotheses about yourself, about other people, and about the world. Check them against the best observations and facts that you can find. Stop being a Pollyanna. Give up pie-in-the-sky. Uproot your easy-to-come-by wishful thinking. Ruthlessly rip up your childish prayers.

Yes, *rip them up!* Again—and again—and again!

Will you never again feel disturbed? I doubt it. Will you reduce your anxiety, depression, and rage to near zero? Probably not.

But I can, almost, just about promise you this: The more scientific, rational, and realistic you become, the less emotionally uptight you will be. Not zero uptight—for that is inhuman or superhuman. But a hell of a lot less. And, as your years go by, and your scientific outlook becomes more solid, less and less neurotic.

Is that a guarantee? No, but a prediction that will probably be fulfilled.

REBT Exercise No. 2

Think of a time when you recently felt anxious about anything. What were you anxious or overconcerned about? Meeting new people? Doing well at work? Winning the approval of a person you liked? Passing a test or a course? Doing well at a job interview? Winning a game of tennis or chess? Getting into a good school? Learning that you have a serious disease? Being treated unfairly?

Look for your command or demand for success or approval that was creating your anxiety or overconcern. What was your *should, ought,* or *must*? Look for these kinds of anxiety-creating thoughts:

"I *must* impress these new people I am meeting."

"Because I *want* to do well at work, I *have* to!"

"Since I like this person very much, I've *got to* win his or her approval!"

"Passing this test or course is very important. Therefore, I *have* to pass it!"

"Because this looks like a good job, *it is necessary* that I please the interviewer."

"If I win this tennis (or chess) game, I will prove how good a player I am. Therefore, *it is essential* that I win it and show everyone that I'm really good!"

"This school that I've applied to is one of the best I could enter, and I really want to get in it. Consequently, I *must* get accepted and it would be *horrible* if I didn't!"

"It would really be *terrible* if I had a serious disease, and if I did I couldn't stand it. I *must* know for certain that I don't have it!"

"I treated these people very well and therefore they *must* not treat me unfairly, and it would be *awful* if they did!"

In every instance where you have recently felt anxious and over-concerned, look for your preferences ("I would very much like to get this job") and then find your command or *must* ("Therefore, I *have* to get it and I *couldn't bear it* if I don't!").

Do the same for your recent feelings of depression. Find what you are depressed about, then persist till you find your *should, ought,* or *must* that is creating your depression. Take a look at these examples:

"Because I want this job and *should have* prepared for the interview and didn't prepare as well as I *must,* I'm an *idiot* who doesn't *deserve* a good job like this!"

"I could have practiced more to win this tennis match but didn't practice as much as I *should* have, and that proves that I'm a lazy slob who will *never* be very good at tennis or anything else!"

Find your *shoulds, oughts,* and *musts* that recently made you feel quite angry at someone about some event. For example:

"After I went out of my way to lend John money, he never paid it back, as he absolutely *should* have! What an irresponsible louse he is! He *must* not treat me that way!"

"I could have gone to the beach on Saturday, but foolishly waited until Sunday—when it rained. The weather *should* have continued to be good on Sunday. How *horrible* it was that it rained. I *can't stand* rain when I want to go to the beach!"

Assume that most times when you feel anxious, depressed, or angry you are not only strongly *desiring* but also *commanding* that something go well and that you get what you want. *Cherchez le* should, *cherchez le* must! Look for your *should*, look for your *must*! Don't give up until you find it. If you have trouble finding it, seek the help of a friend, relative, or REBT therapist who will help you find it. Persist!

Also! Assume that your shoulds and musts are, when they defeat you, held *strongly, emotionally*. And assume that you *persistently act* on the basis of them. ("Since I cannot be sure, as I must be, that I can win at tennis, what's the use? I might as well avoid playing it.") You not only *think* destructive musts, you strongly *feel* and *act* on them. You think, feel, and behave in a *must*urbatory manner. All three! But thinking, feeling, and acting can be changed. If you see and attack them!

4

How to Think Scientifically About
Yourself, Other People, and Your
Life Conditions

Let us suppose that I have now sold you on using the scientific method to help yourself overcome your anxiety and to lead a happier existence. Now what? How can you specifically apply science to your relations with yourself, with others, and with the world around you? Read on!

Science, as I pointed out in the previous chapter, is flexible and nondogmatic. It sticks to facts and to reality (which always can change) and to logical thinking (which does not contradict itself and hold two opposite views at the same time). But it also avoids rigid all-or-none and either/or thinking and sees that reality is often two sided and includes contradictory events and characteristics.

Thus, in my relations with you, I am not a totally *good person* or a *bad person* but a *person who* sometimes treats you well and sometimes treats you badly. Instead of viewing world events in a rigid, absolute way, science assumes that such events, and especially human affairs, usually follow the laws of probability.

Here are the main rules of the scientific method:

1. We had better accept what is going on (WIGO) in the world as "reality," even when we don't like it and are trying to change it. We constantly observe and check "facts" to see

21

whether they are still "true" or whether they have changed. We call our observing and checking reality the empirical method of science.

2. We state scientific laws, theories, and hypotheses in a logical, consistent way and avoid important, basic contradictions (as well as false or unrealistic "facts"). We can change these theories when they are not supported by facts or logic.

3. Science is flexible and nonrigid. It is skeptical of all ideas that hold that anything is absolutely, unconditionally, or certainly true—that is, true under all conditions for all time. It willingly revises and changes its theories as new information arises.

4. Science does not uphold any theories or views that cannot be falsified in some manner (for example, the idea that invisible, all-powerful devils exist and cause all the evils in the world). It doesn't claim that the supernatural does not exist, but since there is no way to prove that superhuman beings do or do not exist, it does not include them in the realm of science. Our *beliefs* in supernatural things are important and can be scientifically investigated, and we can often find natural explanations for "supernatural" events. But it is unlikely that we will ever prove or disprove the "reality" of superhuman beings.

5. Science is skeptical that the universe includes "deservingness" and "undeservingness" and that it deifies people (and things) for their "good" acts or damns them for their "bad" behavior. It does not have any absolute, universal standard of "good" and "bad" behavior and assumes that if any group sees certain deeds as "good" it will *tend to* (but doesn't *have to*) reward those who act that way and will *often* (but not *always*) penalize those who act "badly."

6. In regard to human affairs and conduct, science again does not have any absolute rules, but once people establish a standard or goal—such as remaining alive and living happily in social groups—science can study what people are like, the conditions under which they live, and the ways in which they usually act; it can to some extent judge whether they are meeting those goals and whether it might be wise to modify them or to es-

tablish other ways to achieve them. In regard to emotional health and happiness, once people decide their goals and standards (which is not easy for them to do!), science can often help them achieve these aims. But it gives no guarantees! Science can tell us how we probably—but not *certainly*—can have a good life.

If these are some of the main rules of the scientific method, how can you follow them and thereby help yourself be emotionally healthier and happier?

Answer: By taking your emotional upsets, and the irrational Beliefs (iBs) that you mainly use to create them, and by using the scientific method to rip them up. By scientifically thinking, feeling, and acting against them.

To show you how you can do this, let us take some common irrational commands and scientifically examine them.

IRRATIONAL BELIEF

"Because I strongly prefer to do so, I *must* act competently."

SCIENTIFIC ANALYSIS

Is this belief realistic and factual? Obviously not. Because I am a human with some degree of choice, I don't *have to* act competently and can choose to act badly. Moreover, since I am *fallible*, even if I choose always to act competently, I clearly have no way of always doing so.

Is this belief logical? No, because my fallibility contradicts the demand that I *always* must act competently. Also, it doesn't logically follow, from my strong *preferences* to do so, that I *have to* do so.

Is this belief flexible and unrigid? No, it says that under *all* conditions and in *all* ways, I must act competently. It is therefore an *un*-flexible, rigid belief.

Can this belief be falsified? In one way, yes. Because I can prove that I do *not* have to behave competently at all times. But the belief that I *must* act competently implies that I am a supernatural being whose desire for competence must *always* be fulfilled and who has the power to fulfill it.

There may be no way to fully falsify this godlike command, because even if I at times act incompetently, I can claim that I deliberately did so for some special reason and that I can always, if I will to do so, act competently. I can also say, "God's will be done!"—and that, as a child of God, I don't have to explain why I acted "incompetently."

Does this belief prove deservingness? No, this again is an idea that cannot, except by fiat, be proven or disproven. I can legitimately hold that because I am intelligent and because I try hard, I will *usually* or *probably* act competently. But I cannot show that because of my intelligence, my hard work, my aliveness, my desire to succeed, or anything else, the universe undoubtedly *owes* me competence. That kind of obligation, deservingness, or necessity clearly doesn't exist—or else, once again, I *would* always be competent.

Does this belief show that I will act well and get good, happy results by holding it? Definitely not. If I act competently all the time, I may actually get bad results—because many people may be jealous of me, hate me, and try to harm me for being so perfect. And if I rigidly believe that "because I strongly prefer to do so, I *must* act competently." I will at times see that I do not act as well as I presumably must, and will therefore tend to hate myself and the world and make myself anxious and depressed. So this idea won't work—unless I somehow manage to always act quite competently!

IRRATIONAL BELIEF

"I *have to* be approved by people whom I find important, and it's *awful* and *catastrophic* if I am not!"

SCIENTIFIC ANALYSIS

Is this belief realistic and factual? Clearly not, because there is no law of the universe that says that I *have to* be approved of by people whom I find important, and there is a law of probability that says that many of the people I would prefer to approve of me definitely will not. It's not *awful* or *catastrophic* when I am not approved of, only uncomfortable. Bad things may happen to me when I am not approved of. But when something is "awful" it is (a) exceptionally bad, (b) totally bad, or (c) as bad as it could be. Being disapproved of by important people may not even be exceptionally but only moderately bad. It is certainly not totally bad—and it could always be worse. So this belief doesn't by any means conform to reality.

Is this belief logical? No, for just because I find certain people important, it does not follow that they *must* approve of me. And even if I find it highly inconvenient when important people do not approve of me, it doesn't follow that my life will be *catastrophic* or *awful*. Indeed, if someone I like does not quickly like me, I may actually gain: for this person might first like me and later frustrate or leave me.

Is this belief flexible and unrigid? Definitely not, because it holds that under *all* conditions and at *all* times people whom I find important absolutely have to approve of me. Quite inflexible!

Can this belief be falsified? Yes, because important people *can* disapprove of me and I can *still* find life desirable. But it also implies omniscience on my part, since I am *commanding* that people whom I find important must under all conditions approve of me; even when they don't approve, I can *view* them as approving or contend that they really *do* approve, even when the facts show that they most probably don't. I can always claim that I *am* omniscient and that I know people's secret thoughts and feelings; and this kind of belief is falsifiable.

Does this belief prove deservingness? No, I cannot prove that even if I act nicely to important people that there is a rule of the universe that they *ought to* and *have to* approve of me. Deservingness is another falsifiable belief.

Does this belief show that I will act well and get good, happy results by holding it? On the contrary. No matter how hard I try to get people to approve of me, I can easily fail—and if I then think that they *have to* like me, I will most probably feel depressed. By holding the idea that at all times under all conditions people whom I find important *must* approve of me, I will almost certainly fail to work effectively at getting their approval and also hate them, hate myself, and hate the world when they do not do what they supposedly *must*.

Irrational belief

"People have to treat me considerately and fairly, and when they don't they are rotten individuals who deserve to be severely damned and punished."

Scientific analysis

Is this belief realistic and factual? No, it isn't. It commands that under all conditions and at all times other people have to treat me considerately and fairly. Obviously, they don't and the facts of life often prove that they won't. It is also not factual that they are rotten individuals—for such people would be rotten to the core, would never do good or neutral acts, and would be eternally doomed to act rottenly. No such *totally* rotten people seem to exist. This belief also implies that people who treat me inconsiderately and unfairly *always* deserve to be severely punished and that somehow their damnation and punishment *will be* arranged. This is not what happens in reality.

Is this belief logical? No, because it implies that because people sometimes do treat me inconsiderately and unfairly, they are totally rotten individuals and always deserve to be punished. Even if I can indubitably prove that by usual human standards some people treat me badly, I cannot prove that *therefore* they are totally rotten and *therefore* always deserve to be punished. Such conclusions do not follow from my empirical observations that people treat me badly.

Is this belief flexible and unrigid? No, because it states and implies that in every single case *all* people who treat me inconsiderately and unfairly are *totally* rotten and *invariably* deserve to be severely damned and punished. No exceptions!

Can this belief be falsified? Part of it can be because it holds that people who treat me badly and unjustly are totally rotten individuals, and it can be shown they often do some good and neutral acts. My belief in deservingness and damnation, however, cannot be falsified, because even if no one else upheld me and believed it to be true, I could always claim that all the other people in the world were sadly mistaken, that my view of punishment and damnation is unquestionably the right one, and that punishment for those who treat me unfairly *should* exist, even when it doesn't. When people who wrong me are, in fact, not severely punished, I can always contend that there are special reasons why they have not been penalized so far and that they undoubtedly will be in the future or in some afterlife.

Does this belief system prove deservingness? No, even if people treat me inconsiderately and unfairly, and even when they sometimes are punished after they do so, I cannot prove that (a) they were punished *because* they treated me badly, (b) that some universal fate or being *dooms* them to this punishment, or (c) that hereafter they (and other people like them) will *always* be damned and doomed for treating me (and others) unjustly. I will even have trouble proving that their acts against me indubitably *are* bad—because in some respects they may be "good" and because some others may not view them as "bad." The concept of deservingness for one's "sins" implies that certain acts are unquestionably under all conditions "sinful." And this is impossible to prove.

Does having this belief mean that I will act well and get good, happy results by holding it? Not at all! If I strongly believe that people have to treat me considerately and fairly, that they are rotten individuals when they don't, and that they then deserve to be severely damned and punished, I will very likely bring on several unfortunate results:

1. I will feel very angry and vindictive, and will consequently stir up my nervous system and my body in a way that will often prove harmful to me.
2. I will be obsessed with the people whom I think have done me in and will spend enormous amounts of time and energy thinking about them.
3. When I try to do something about people's unfair acts, I will tend to be so enraged that I will fight with them in a frantic manner and will often fail to convince them or stop them.

Indeed, they are likely to see *me* as an overly enraged, and therefore unfair, person and deliberately resist acknowledging their wrongdoing.

4. I will probably be unable to understand why people treat me "wrongly," may unjustly or paranoically accuse them of wrongs that they have not committed, and will often interfere with my amicably and objectively discussing with them and perhaps arranging for suitable compromises.

If you resort to scientifically questioning and challenging your own irrational Beliefs, as shown in the above examples, you will tend to see that they are unrealistic, distinctly illogical, often inflexible and rigid, cannot be falsified, and are based on false concepts of universal deservingness. If you continue to hold these unrealistic and illogical notions, you will frequently sabotage your own interests.

This kind of analysis and disputing of your irrational Beliefs (iBs) is one of the main methods of REBT. If you continue to use it, you will take advantage of the most powerful antidote to human misery that has so far been invented: scientific thinking. Science will not absolutely *guarantee* that you can stubbornly refuse to make yourself miserable about anything. But it will greatly help!

REBT Exercise No. 3

Whenever you feel seriously upset (anxious, depressed, enraged, self-hating, or self-pitying), or are probably behaving against your own basic interest (avoiding what you had better do or addicted to acts that you'd better not do), assume that you are thinking unscientifically. Look for these common ways in which you (and practically all your friends and relatives) deny the rules of science:

UNREALISTIC THINKING THAT DENIES THE FACTS OF LIFE

Examples

"If I am nice to people, they will surely love me and treat me well."

"If I don't pass this test, I'll never get through school and will end up as a bum or a bag lady."

Illogical and contradictory beliefs

Examples
"Because I strongly want you to love me, you have to do so."

"When I fail at a job interview, that proves that I'm hopeless and will never get a good job."

"People must treat me fairly even when I am unkind and unjust to them."

Unprovable and unfalsifiable beliefs

Examples
"Because I have harmed others, I am doomed to roast in hell and suffer for eternity."

"I am a special person who will always come out on top no matter what I do."

"I have a magical ability to make people do what I want them to do."

"Because I strongly feel that you hate me, it is certain that you do."

Beliefs in deservingness or undeservingness

Examples
"Because I am a good person, I deserve to succeed in life, and fate will make sure that nice things will happen to me."

"Because I have not done as well as I could, I deserve to suffer and get nowhere in life."

Assumptions that your strong beliefs (and the feelings that go with them) will bring good results and lead to comfort and happiness

Examples
"Because you treated me unfairly, as you *should* not have done, my

making myself angry at you will make you treat me better and make me happier."

"If I thoroughly condemn myself for acting stupidly, that will make me act better in the future."

When you have discovered some of your unscientific beliefs with which you are creating emotional problems and making yourself act against your own interests, use the scientific method to challenge and dispute them. Ask yourself:

Is this belief realistic? Is it opposed to the facts of life?

Is this belief logical? Is it contradictory to itself or to my other beliefs?

Can I prove this belief? Can I falsify it?

Does this belief prove that the universe has a law of deservingness or undeservingness? If I act well, do I completely deserve a good life, and if I act badly, do I totally deserve a bad existence?

If I continue to strongly hold the belief (and to have the feelings and do the acts it often creates), will I perform well, get the results I want to get, and lead a happier life? Or will holding it tend to make me less happy?

Persist at using the scientific method of questioning and challenging your irrational Beliefs until you begin to give them up, increase your effectiveness, and enjoy yourself more.

5

Why the Usual Kinds of Insight Won't Help You Overcome Your Emotional Problems

Will insight into your emotional problems help you overcome them? It may help—providing it is not conventional or psychoanalytic insight.

Conventional insight will help you very little. For it says that your knowledge of exactly how you got disturbed will make you less neurotic. Drivel! It will often help make you become nutti*er*!

Suppose, for example, your parents insisted that you make a million dollars, else you are a slob. Suppose you have actually made little money and you now "therefore" feel worthless. Your wonderful "insight" about the "origin" of your self-hatred may only push you to loathe your parents. Or to hate yourself more for listening to them! Or to think that they were right—that you *should* have made a million dollars and are a turd for not following their great teachings.

Insight, even when it is correct, doesn't automatically *make* you better, though—if you *use* it correctly—it may help. And it can easily—very easily!—be false. For even if you did take your self-hating idea from your parents, we still had better ask: *Why* did you accept these ideas? What are you *now* doing to carry them on? How do we know that if your parents taught you to always accept yourself, you *still* wouldn't have concluded that you must make a million dollars to be worthwhile?

In other words, conventional "insight" is usually dubious and hardly tells you what factors *really* caused your disturbance. Nor what you can *do* to overcome it.

Psychoanalytic insight is worse. Because it is based on many different and contradictory guesses—and they cannot possibly all be true. Thus, if you now believe that you absolutely *must* make a million dollars to accept yourself, different analysts will try to convince you that you believe this because:

1. Your mother gave you pleasurable enemas and you are therefore "anally fixated" and are obsessed with money.
2. You unconsciously think that a bag of money represents your genitals and therefore your obsession with money really means that you want promiscuous sex.
3. Your father was cruel to you, so now you have to win his love and think you can do so only by making a million dollars.
4. You hate your father and want to shame him by making more money than he made.
5. You have a small penis or bosom and have to make lots of money to compensate for it.
6. Your unconscious views money as power and you really are obsessed with gaining power, not money.
7. Your great-grandfather was a pauper and you now have to remove the family shame about this by becoming a millionaire.

Et cetera, et cetera.

All these psychoanalytic interpretations—and a thousand similar ones—are possible, but none of them is very plausible. And even if one of these "insights" were true, how would knowing it help you *change* your obsession about making money?

If, for example, you truly think you have to win your father's love and that you can only do so by making a million dollars, how does that knowledge make you surrender your dire need for his approval? To change, you still would have to *dispute* that idea and to *act* against it. And psychoanalysis helps you do nothing like this—and encourages you (and your analyst) to keep looking for more brilliant "true" interpretations.

Conventional and psychoanalytic "insights," then, are not enough—or are too much. They frequently block scientific thinking and prevent active change. Does REBT therefore ignore insight? Not at all! It uses—and teaches—several kinds of *un*conventional insight that help you understand your emotional problems and what you can specifically *do* to uproot them.

In REBT terms, insight first means understanding who you are. Actually, you *are* a human being who *has* various likes and dislikes and who *does* many acts to get more of what you like and less of what you dislike. So REBT helps you explore your likes and dislikes and what you can do to achieve the former and avoid the latter.

REBT, then, helps you not only to understand what you "are" but to *change* what you harmfully think, feel, and do. It accepts your desires, wishes, preferences, goals, and values, then tries to help you achieve them. But REBT shows you how to separate your *preferences* from your *insistences*—and thus keep from sabotaging your own goals. It gives you insight into what you are now doing rather than into what you (and your damned parents!) have done.

Annabel, one of my clients who cherished her perfectionism because she felt that it made her a fine writer and an excellent mother, was having a hard time with some of David Burns's teachings against perfectionism in his book, *Feeling Good*. Dr. Burns, she thought, told her to give up all ideal goals and stick only to realistic and average ones. Then she couldn't be disappointed or depressed.

"But if I don't strive for ideal goals, I will never achieve half the good things I do achieve," she said. "How about *that*?"

"True," I replied. "You and many outstanding inventors and writers have striven for the ideal and have thereby helped yourself do remarkably well. REBT, therefore, does not oppose competition or striving for outstanding achievement. It advocates *task*-perfection, not *self*-perfection."

"What does that mean?"

"It means that you can try to be as good, or even as perfect, as you can—at any *project* or *task*. You can try to make *it* ideal. But *you* are not a good person if *it* is perfect. You are still a *person who* completed a perfect project, but never a *good person* for doing so."

"How, then, do I become an incompetent or bad person?"

"You don't! When you do incompetent or evil *acts*, you become a *person who acted badly*—never a *bad person*."

"But why, then, should I strive for perfection—or even for good achievements?"

"Because you presumably find *them*—the achievements—desirable. And if your achievements are outstanding or ideal, you will find them *more* desirable—more enjoyable. But your achievements, no matter how good, never make you a totally *good person*."

"But isn't Burns right about my being disappointed if I try for the ideal and don't reach it?"

"Yes—disappointed, but not self-hating if you use REBT."

"And how do I do that?"

"By not giving up your *preference* for perfect motherhood or perfect writing, but eliminating your *demands*, or *musts*. As long as you tell yourself, 'I really would *like* to write a perfect novel—but I don't *have to*,' you'll retain your task-perfectionism but not your *self-perfectionism*."

"So the crucial difference is the *must*. I can strive for perfectionism in my writing as long as I don't think I *must* achieve it and do not view myself as a sleazy writer and a rotten person if I don't."

"Exactly!"

Annabel continued to work hard at perfecting her mothering and her writing. But she overcame the anxiety that drove her to therapy by changing her perfectionist *musts* back to *preferences*.

REBT at times deals with your past—for if you are disturbed, you most likely had crooked thinking then as well as now. But it mainly shows what *you* did and what *you* thought in your early years—and spends little time on what your dear parents and others did to you. It especially shows you how you are *now* thinking, feeling, and acting—and how to *change* your weaknesses.

Insight, then, can help you see exactly how you are sabotaging

WHY THE USUAL KINDS OF INSIGHTS WON'T HELP 35

yourself and what you can do to change. REBT—which uses philosophy more than most other forms of therapy—stresses many different kinds of self-understanding. The following chapters will describe many insights that REBT teaches and how you can use them in your efforts to stubbornly refuse to make yourself miserable about practically anything.

REBT Exercise No. 4

Try to remember some of the worst incidents that took place during your childhood. How about the time your mother bawled you out in front of several of your friends? Or the time you were called upon to recite in class and were so panicked that you couldn't say anything and the whole class laughed at you. Or the time when your skirt or pants were hung too low and half of your behind was sticking out for everyone to see. Or the occasion when you told another child how much you really liked him or her and got only a cold or negative response.

Do you remember that very "traumatic" event or events? Do you still think that it greatly influenced the rest of your life?

Well, it really didn't! Not if you think about it carefully.

First of all, try to remember—or to figure out—what you told yourself to make this past event so "traumatic" and "hurtful." When your mother bawled you out in front of your friends, weren't you telling yourself that she *shouldn't* have done that and that you *couldn't stand* your friends' knowing something negative about you? When you were panicked about reciting in class, weren't you thinking, "I *must* answer my teacher well. Isn't it *awful* when I do poorly—and when the other kids laugh at me!" When you neglected to hitch up your skirt or pants and your behind was showing, weren't you telling yourself, "How shameful to be so careless about my clothing! I *must* not behave so foolishly!"

Track down—as you definitely can—the irrational Beliefs that *made* you feel hurt and upset when you were young. Then also look for the self-defeating ideas that you have *kept* repeating to yourself since that time and that have made you *keep* this "traumatic" incident alive.

Such as: "My own mother knew I was no good and that's why she kept criticizing me. She was right!" "I *still* can't recite well in front of people. How terrible!" "Because I dressed so sloppily as a child, everyone could see what a slob I was. And I still haven't improved, as I *should*. I am a fool who *deserves* to have others laugh at me!"

Use your knowledge of REBT, and of how you upset yourself with your *musts* and commands, to understand exactly *how* you upset yourself during your childhood and how you are *still* preserving your upset feelings today.

6

REBT Insight No. 1: Making Yourself Fully Aware of Your Healthy and Unhealthy Feelings

Insight is another name for awareness. Awareness is the first step toward ridding yourself of misery. The more you are keenly aware of your misery-creating thoughts, feelings, and behaviors, the greater your chances are of ridding yourself of them.

Let us—as we usually do in REBT—begin with your miserable feelings. How can you be aware of what you feel—and how healthy your feelings are?

The first part of this question is fairly easy to answer: You know how you feel by merely asking yourself, "How do I feel?"

You sometimes may, of course, be defensive. You may deny that you feel anxious or angry because you are ashamed to admit such "wrong" feelings.

Usually, however, you won't. If you are severely anxious or depressed, you will tend to feel so uncomfortable that you will freely admit—at least to yourself!—that you have these miserable feelings. Such misery is easy to feel—and to acknowledge.

But how *healthy* are your uncomfortable emotions? Oh, that's a much harder question to answer. But REBT gives you a pretty good key. For it is the one system of psychotherapy that clearly distinguishes between healthy and unhealthy feelings.

How? By stressing Insight No. 1: *You create both healthy and unhealthy feelings when your goals and desires are blocked.*

You can—and had better—learn how to clearly distinguish between these self-induced emotional reactions. Most other therapies—such as the behavior therapy of Joseph Wolpe and the cognitive therapies of Richard Lazarus, Aaron Beck, and Donald Meichenbaum—emphasize strong feelings, like severe sadness and irritation, and put them into the same category as feelings of depression and anger.

Not so REBT! REBT considers your strong feelings of sadness, irritation, and concern to be healthy, because they help you to express your displeasure at undesirable happenings and to work at modifying them. But REBT defines your feelings of depression, anger, and anxiety as (almost always) harmful, because they stem from your unrealistic commands that unpleasant events absolutely *must* not exist, and because they usually interfere with your changing these events when they do exist.

Unlike most other therapies, therefore, REBT shows you not only how to get in touch with your negative (and your positive) feelings, but also how to be aware of—to have *insight* into—whether they are healthy or unhealthy. It encourages you to feel your feelings—and *also* to weigh how desirable they are. Do you really *want* to feel them? And what good or bad results do they get you?

Thus, if you feel concerned about losing your job, you will try to be on time, to work hard, and to cooperate with your boss and your associates. If, however, you are *over*concerned—or severely worried—about losing it, you will tend to be obsessed with it, *take away* time and energy from doing it, and lose confidence that you *can* perform it adequately.

Result? No damned job! Or a job and an ulcer. Or great misery while working.

Again: If you are disappointed and regretful about being rejected by a love partner, you will try to discover why you were abandoned, to win back that person's love, or to attempt to mate with a more suitable partner. But if you are angry at your rejector, you will probably antagonize him or her and remain an enemy instead of a friend.

And if you are depressed about being rejected, you will tend to withdraw completely and see yourself as quite unlovable.

Your feelings of disappointment and regret, then, are usually healthy feelings that help you withstand undesirable events and strive for a happier future. Panic, depression, and rage, on the other hand, are unhealthy feelings that interfere with your coping and block your improving of your life.

How about *mild* or *moderate* anxiety or anger? Don't *those* feelings spur you to act against life's hassles? Aren't *they* therefore beneficial?

Not exactly. Almost any negative feeling occasionally can be useful. Extreme panic may energize you to outrun a forest fire. Intense rage may help you fight against an unfair bureaucracy.

May! But they probably won't!

Extreme panic will *usually* disorganize and freeze you so that you won't efficiently escape from the fire. Intense rage will *normally* make you *stew* instead of *do* when you encounter unfairness, and if you act while enraged you will often fight foolishly and badly.

You have, moreover, better choices. You can choose to be strongly concerned rather than grippingly panicked about escaping from a fire and you can decide to be greatly *displeased* and *determined to act against* unfairness.

With, most probably, better results! And with, almost certainly, less dreadful wear on your system!

REBT holds that you can choose between great concern about your safety or panic or horror about it. And REBT contends that you can decide to be strongly *displeased about* and *determined to change* injustice or rashly infuriated about it.

And you'd better be concerned about unpleasant happenings. For your feelings of concern, caution, care, and vigilance help keep you safe and satisfied; whereas your feelings of overconcern, anxiety, panic, and horror help keep you insecure and dissatisfied. Similarly, when you are treated unfairly or badly, you can choose to feel healthily displeased, sorry, frustrated, and determined to change the unfair situation. Or you can choose to feel unhealthily angry, enraged, furious, and homicidal—and consequently whining and *in*active.

Can you clearly distinguish between unhealthy and healthy feelings? Not always, since your emotions are rarely pure and often include healthy and unhealthy elements. At one and the same time, you can be rationally *concerned* about escaping from a fire and irrationally *over*concerned or panicked about escaping. Where does the first feeling end and the second one begin?

REBT has an answer. It holds that when you are healthily concerned about any danger, you are sensibly *desiring, wishing,* or *preferring* to avoid it. But when you are overconcerned, panicked, or horrified about the same danger, you are still desiring but *also* insisting that you absolutely *must*—yes, *have to*—avoid it. You *legitimately* and *wisely* desire to avoid danger. Because why should you not *want* what you want and why should you not *prefer* to avoid what you don't want?

No reason! But your dogmatic command that you always *must* get what you desire is illegitimate and self-defeating—because the universe clearly does not *owe* you your heart's desire. And you will interfere with getting your preferences by fanatically demanding that they *have to be* fulfilled.

I have said that REBT is more philosophic than other systems of psychotherapy. Now perhaps you can see how it is. When you are disturbed, REBT's Insight No. 1 holds that you have both healthy and unhealthy emotions. Usually (not always!) you can distinguish between the two by looking for the cognitions—the thoughts and feelings—that accompany them.

Your healthy feelings arise from thoughts that express your preferences—such as, "I strongly *want* to avoid this fire but I don't *have to* escape and live happily ever after." And: "I abhor injustice and am determined to fight against it."

Unhealthy feelings stem from *commanding, dictatorial* thoughts—such as, "I *absolutely must* avoid this fire because the universe ordains that I *have to* live and be happy!" And: "I hate everyone who acts unjustly! They *absolutely must not* behave that way! At all costs, I *have to* stop them and make them see that they *must* always treat me fairly!"

Insight No. 1 of REBT, once again, states: "You create both healthy and unhealthy feelings when your goals and desires are blocked; and you can, and had better, learn how to clearly distinguish between these two self-created emotional reactions." By using the ABCs of REBT—which are outlined in the next chapter—you can learn how to do this.

REBT Exercise No. 5

Go back to the end of chapter 2 and once again do the REBT exercise that gives you practice in distinguishing between your healthy and unhealthy negative feelings. Also try to see the difference between some of your healthy and unhealthy positive feelings.

Imagine that you are performing something remarkably well—for example, playing tennis, acting, writing, painting, or running a business in an outstanding manner. Let yourself feel happy about this accomplishment.

Now observe your happy feeling. Is it only a feeling of being happy and pleased about *it*, your performance? Or do you also—be honest now!—feel great about *you*, about *yourself*, about your *whole being*? Do you feel like a *great person*—a noble, godlike, almost *superhuman individual*?

If you do feel like a noble, superhuman, holier-than-thou *person*, you are then, according to REBT, experiencing an *un*healthy positive feeling. For you are then in a grandiose, egotistical state and have raised yourself above other human beings. You have jumped from the idea that "My behavior is outstanding" to "I am therefore an outstanding, great person!"

This is dangerous. Because when you *don't* perform remarkably well the next time, back to slobhood you will go! And even when you do perform well, you will be anxious about *not* doing so next time. So you had better like your fine *performance*—but not deify *yourself* for doing it.

When you do feel godlike or noble, look for your *shoulds* and *musts*. Such as: "I have just done as well as I *have to* do. Good. My success makes me a fine, worthy individual." And: "Now that I have done this thing so well, people will see me as a marvelous person. I *need* them to see me in that light in order to accept myself and be happy with my life."

When you feel unhealthily bad or great, make a list of the disadvantages of having these feelings. You will find it easy to list the disadvantages of negative feelings, like those of depression, guilt, or self-hatred. But your positive unhealthy feelings also have distinct disadvantages. Thus, when you feel like a great and superior *person*, here is a list of disadvantages these feelings may bring you.

- Unrealistically assuming that you will always continue to perform well
- Acting in an egotistical, arrogant, and obnoxious manner to others
- Thinking that you are so great that you do not have to bother to work at performing well in the future
- Being anxious about later falling on your face and greatly disappointing others who admire you
- Maintaining and increasing your belief that you *have to do* well and that it is *terrible* if you don't
- Making too much of the tasks at which you do well and neglecting other aspects of your life
- Becoming so absorbed in your own ego that you lose your feelings for and misunderstanding of others and ruin your human relationships
- Striving so hard to continue to perform well that you put yourself under great stress and possibly interfere with your mental and physical health

Ask yourself whether you are bringing on any of these—or other—disadvantages by making yourself feel unhealthy positive (or negative) feelings. If so, look again for the demands and commands with which you are creating these self-defeating feelings and work at disputing them and giving them up.

7

REBT Insight No. 2: You Control Your Emotional Destiny

Many modern therapies—particularly psychoanalysis—let people cop out on their responsibility for their own neuroses. Not REBT. Over twenty years ago, *Psychology Today* titled it, "The No-Cop-Out Therapy"—which indeed it is.

Not that REBT (like some extreme cults) says that you are *totally* responsible for your upsets. You aren't. As noted before, you are influenced by your biology and your learning, which also help you to become disturbed. Nonetheless!—you will, to *some* degree, control your emotional destiny. To *some* extent you choose how often and how intensely you upset your own emotional applecart. For you *listen* to your parents and teachers. You *carry on* their nonsense. You choose to *indulge* in your panic and despair—even when you sometimes know how to stop these feelings.

Yes—*you*.

Which is quite fortunate. For if emotional problems simply overwhelmed you, if outside conditions really *made* you as neurotic as you are, what could you do to help yourself be undisturbed? Damned little!

But if you, no one but you, mainly create your nervous destiny, you most likely can change this destiny. Whatever you *choose* to do, you can also *refuse* to do. Whatever you *choose* to think and feel, you can also *refuse* to think and feel. This is REBT's Insight No. 2: *You largely (not completely) create your own disturbed thoughts and feelings, and therefore you have the power to control and change them. Providing that you accept this insight and work hard at using it!*

Let me outline the famous ABCs of REBT. A stands for Activating Event—which is usually some happening that blocks or frustrates your important goals, desires, or preferences. For example: you want a job and you fail the interview and get rejected. A (Activating Event) is your failure and your rejection.

Please note! In REBT, we start the ABCs of emotional disturbance with your goals, purposes, desires, and values. You *enter* these ABCs with (conscious and unconscious) Goals (G).

What, usually, are your main goals, about which you sometimes make yourself miserable?

They are, first, that you stay alive and, second, that you be satisfied or happy. Once you are born, you have strong biological tendencies to want to remain alive and to strive for contentment. If you didn't have the wish to survive, you rarely would. And if you didn't have the desire—the Goal—of being happy, you would probably not want to keep living. So your Goals of surviving and being happy while you are alive are inborn tendencies and help perpetuate you and your species.

How do you want to be happy or satisfied?

- When you are by yourself, alone?
- When you are with other people?
- When you are intimately involved with a few special people?
- When you are doing well in business or a career and are earning a living?
- When you are involved in art, science, sports, or other recreations and creative acts?

Once you desire to survive and be happy, you bring these Goals to the ABCs of human living. You go to A (Activating Events) wishing, preferring to get your Goals fulfilled; and when you feel miser-

able and act foolishly (at point C, Consequences of A and B), your
Goals are usually being blocked at A.

So now we have:

- G—your Goal of getting what you want (especially, success and
  approval).
- A—the Activating Events that block your Goal (especially, failure
  and rejection).
- C—the Consequences of G and A (especially, feelings of anxiety
  and depression and self-defeating behaviors, like withdrawal and
  addiction).

Whenever your Goals (Gs) are thwarted by unfortunate Activating Events (As) and whenever you feel disturbed at Consequences
(Cs), you tend to falsely blame C on A. Thus, you say, "Because I
failed and got rejected at A and because I then felt depressed at C, A
causes C. Failure and rejection *make me* depressed!"

Wrong! False! Mistaken!

A (failure or rejection that blocks your Goals) *contributes to* but
never really *causes* C.

Why? Because, obviously, if a hundred people with the same
Goal (say, desire to obtain a job) all were blocked at A (got rejected),
would they all feel equally depressed at C? Obviously not.

Some would feel very depressed and suicidal. Some would feel
disappointed and sorry but not really depressed. Some would feel
relaxed or indifferent. A few would even feel happy. Why? Because
these few would conclude that the job they wanted was really unpleasant. Or that they would rather be unemployed than be working.

So, you see, Activating Events (As) do *not* directly cause disturbed
Consequences (Cs) in your gut—though they may contribute to
these feelings.

This is not a new discovery of REBT. Many philosophers have
pointed this out—especially the Greek and Roman stoics, almost
2,500 years ago. One of their outstanding thinkers, Epictetus, put it
clearly in the first century AD: "People are disturbed not by things,

but by the views they take of them." And Shakespeare restated this idea in *Hamlet*: "There's nothing either good or bad but thinking makes it so."

So REBT's view of the ABCs of emotional disturbance has an honorable history. Not that REBT—as you will see later—is pure stoicism. It isn't! But it agrees with Epictetus: You largely (not *entirely*) create your own misery. And you can *choose* not to do so.

How can you prevent and undo your upsetness? By gaining insight into the Bs in the ABCs of REBT.

What are these Bs?

The Bs of REBT are Beliefs-Feelings-Behaviors. REBT calls them Beliefs-Feelings-Behaviors because they include all three processes. But in this book we shall mainly use the term "Beliefs."

You can be aware or unaware, conscious or unconscious of your Beliefs. You can express them in words, images, fantasies, symbols, and various other ways. If you would clearly understand and use them to change yourself, you had better state them consciously and verbally. But you can undo your misery-creating ideas yourself. In fact, one of the virtues of REBT is that it shows you *many* ways of changing your Beliefs—as I shall emphasize in this book:

When you needlessly make yourself miserable, you use two main kinds of Beliefs:

1. RATIONAL BELIEFS (rBs)

Your rBs are thoughts (and feelings and actions) that help you feel healthily and behave effectively—that enable you to get more of what you want and less of what you don't want. They include "cool" thoughts or calm descriptions of what is going on (WIGO) in your life. For example: "This job interviewer is frowning at me and may not favor me for this job." This is a "cool" thought because it tells you what the interviewer is doing but not how you *rate* or *evaluate* his or her act.

You can understand your feelings better if you look for the "warm" thoughts that you include in your rational Beliefs (rBs). For example: "Because I would like to get this job, I dislike this interviewer's frowning at me and wish he would stop frowning and instead beam at me." With these "warm" thoughts you express your desires, wishes, preferences, and dislikes. They *rate* or *evaluate* what is occurring in terms of your basic Goals (G).

"Warm" rational Beliefs are also undogmatic and are based on probability instead of certainty. For example: "There is a good chance that I would like this job if I get it, but I actually may not. And even if I would like it very much, I don't *have to* get it or keep it—though it would be very nice if I did!"

2. Irrational beliefs (iBs)

Your iBs are thoughts (and feelings and actions) that help you feel unhealthy and behave ineffectively—that interfere with your getting more of what you want and less of what you don't want. They start with "cool" thoughts ("This job interviewer seems to dislike me") as well as "warm" thoughts ("I wish he would like me and I hate his disliking me and keeping me from this job"). But they also include "hot" thoughts that strongly rate what is going on and are absolutist, dogmatic, and commanding. For example: "No matter what, I *must* have this interviewer like me and give me this job! If he doesn't it's *awful*! I *can't* stand it! If I lose this job that proves that I am an incompetent, worthless person who will never be able to get and keep a good position!

Note well! REBT does not hold that *all* emotional disturbance stems from iBs, because it may have other important causes. Nor does it claim that all irrational Beliefs lead to disturbance, because (as John Dewey once said) many of them don't. You may irrationally believe, for example, that all women are crazy, that eating turtles will cure warts, and that two and two equal five, and you may not feel miserable. You will probably act inefficiently if you believe these (and a hundred other) irrational Beliefs. But you may or may not disturb yourself by holding them.

REBT merely—and uniquely—contends that when you rigidly hold certain irrational Beliefs—when you dogmatically command that you *must* do well, *have to* be approved by others, *have got to* have people treat you fairly, and always *ought* to live with easy and enjoyable conditions—when you stoutly hold these iBs, you will tend to make yourself needlessly miserable and will probably defeat some of your most cherished goals.

REBT further states that when you hold irrational Beliefs (iBs), you consciously or unconsciously *choose* these absolutist shoulds, oughts, and musts—and therefore you have the ability to consciously explore and change them.

Let me therefore repeat Insight No. 2: *You largely (not completely) create and control your own disturbed thoughts and feelings; and therefore you have the power to radically change them. Providing that you accept this insight and work hard at using it!*

More specifically: You can undo your misery *if* you work at finding and surrendering your irrational Beliefs.

George, who had heard that REBT deals with irrational Beliefs, came to see me because he "irrationally" lusted after almost every woman under forty that he met. George was twenty-five.

I soon showed George that he mainly had a strong *preference* for sex with many women—but that was hardly irrational, as long as it was only that, a preference. His rational Belief (rB) was, "I like sex very much and wish I could have it with most of the women I meet."

His main irrational Belief (iB) was, "I *must* not have such a strong sex preference! I *should* always be more selective in my lusting—and only want to go to bed with women whom I really like."

"Why is this belief irrational?" George asked me when he acknowledged having it.

"Because," I answered, "it's a command rather than a desire. You can rationally prefer to have less desire—even to be without any lust. But once you say to yourself, 'I *must* not desire! I *must* not lust!' you will become obsessed with your desire—and probably experience it more intensely. Moreover, you will not be able to plot and scheme how to diminish it. So your *determination* to be less lustful will get you into trouble. It will tend to make you anxious and guilty."

"It does!" George exclaimed.

"So you'd better see what your irrational Belief really is," I pointed out.

"You mean," said George, "I have an irrational Belief about a rational Belief—about my strong preference for sex. Is that right?"

"Very well put! In REBT terms, you have an iB about an rB. Now if we can help you to give up your irrational Belief that you *must* not be lustful, you will still have the rational Belief that sex can be very enjoyable, and will probably be able to engage in more sex—and enjoy it thoroughly!"

"I see!" said George.

But although it was easy for him, with my help, to see the difference between his rB and his iB, he at first had trouble eliminating the latter. For he correctly asked himself, at D (Disputing of irrational Beliefs), "Why *must* I not lust after many women? Why is it wrong for me to do so?" And he correctly answered, "It's okay for me to have strong sex drives. Therefore, I'm okay as a person."

This was a wrong answer because he soon went back to thinking: "But suppose it *is* wrong for me to be so sexy? Other men aren't as hungry as I am. So maybe I'm abnormal in that respect. And if I am, that makes me a pretty lousy person!"

When George came up with this answer—and still remained anxious and guilty—I showed him that he had a highly inelegant solution to his guilt problem and that a more elegant REBT solution would be for him *first* to show himself that his preference, "I would like to have sex with many women," was rational. But second, he had better also understand that even if his sex desires were unusual, and if too much indulgence in them was irrational, that would only mean that he was a *person who* had "abnormal" desires but *not* an "*abnormal*" *or lousy person*. For REBT shows people how to stop damning and to fully accept *themselves* even when some of their acts are stupid, wrong, or immoral.

Anyway, when George saw the difference between his rational and irrational Beliefs and when he kept working to surrender the latter, he finally became unanxious and unguilty about his strong sex drives. And one time, when he foolishly spent several weeks compulsively having sex with several women while sadly neglecting his retail business, he was able to conclude that his behavior was stupid and self-defeating but that he was not a *stupid, rotten person*. After that, he was able to handle his promiscuous desires more reasonably.

By understanding—and working at—Insight No. 2, George was able to control his emotional destiny. And sometimes to feel sorry but not depressed about his compulsive sex acts.

REBT Exercise No. 6

Try to remember a recent time in which you felt anxious about something—such as feeling anxious or panicked about taking a test, playing in an important game, or asking for a promotion or a raise at work. Assume that you created this anxious feeling by thinking (a) a rational Belief (rB) or *preference* and (b) an irrational Belief (iB) or strong *demand*.

Example of your rB or preference: "I would very much like to pass this test, but if I don't I can try to pass it later. And if I never pass it, I still can live and be happy."

Example of your iB or demand: "I have to pass this test, and if I don't I'll be a truly stupid person who will *never* be able to get what I really want."

Think, now, of a recent time when you felt depressed about a failure or a rejection. Assume, again, that you created this depressed feeling by telling yourself rational Beliefs (rBs) and irrational Beliefs (iBs). Find them!

Example of your rB or preference: "I strongly wanted to win that game but I can accept losing it and learn to play better next time. I can also enjoy playing even if I lose many games."

Example of your iB or demand: "I absolutely *ought* to have won that game and because I lost it I am a thoroughly rotten player and an incompetent person."

Think of a time when you became angry or enraged. Assume, once again, that you *made yourself* angry by holding both a rational Belief (rB) or *preference* and an irrational Belief (iB) or *godlike command*.

Example of your rB or preference: "I would have very much liked my boss seeing that I deserved a raise and giving me a good one.

Since he didn't, he unfortunately doesn't appreciate my work and that's too bad, but hardly the end of the world."

Example of your iB or godlike command: "Because I am a good worker, my boss absolutely *should have* appreciated me and given me a good raise. Since he didn't, he's no damned good and deserves to lose his rotten business!"

Keep looking for and persist until you find your rational Beliefs (rBs) and irrational Beliefs (iBs) whenever you feel anxious, depressed, enraged, self-downing, and self-pitying. Try to see that your rBs just about always express your preferences and distastes—what you want and don't want—and that your iBs express your unconditional musts, shoulds, and oughts—your godlike demands and commands on yourself, others, and on the universe. Practice seeing this difference many times until you easily and automatically tend to clearly see it. Work at fully accepting the reality that however legitimate and appropriate your goals and wishes are, they are hardly the same as your dogmatic and needless demands.

8

REBT Insight No. 3: The Tyranny of the Shoulds

What main specific irrational Beliefs (iBs) do you use to upset yourself? You probably adopt and invent many of them, as we shall keep revealing in this book.

Your most important irrational pathway is *mus*turbation—or your devoutly following of what Karen Horney called "the tyranny of the shoulds."

Following Horney's lead, we arrive at Insight No. 3: *You mainly make yourself needlessly and neurotically miserable by strongly holding absolutist irrational Beliefs (iBs), especially by rigidly believing unconditional shoulds, oughts, and musts.*

How do you acquire or invent your destructive musts?

Very easily! As a human, you are first of all born suggestible—gullible—to the commandments of your parents and your culture. Worse yet, you have your own genius for inventing rules and regulations that you rigidly believe that you (and others) *have to* follow.

You, like virtually all humans, are a natural-born reasoner and problem solver. But you are also a master of rationalization, self-delusion, and bigotry.

You think straightly—and crookedly. In fact, you are sane enough to keep yourself alive and happy—and you are crazy enough to be irrational, illogical, and inconsistent. As the long history of humanity clearly shows!

You so easily think foolishly that your thoughts often bring on emotional problems. I described twelve major irrational beliefs in my first paper on Rational Emotive Behavior Therapy that I gave in 1956 at the American Psychological Association's annual convention in Chicago.

Psychologists soon became so enthusiastic about these irrational Beliefs (iBs) that they devised several tests of irrationality and have now published hundreds of studies using these tests. Over 90 percent of these studies support the REBT theory that emotionally disturbed people subscribe to more irrational ideas than do less disturbed individuals.

Following my lead, a number of other therapists created tests of crooked thinking (such as the Beck Depression Inventory) and have used them in hundreds of research studies. Again, the results almost always show that disturbed people subscribe to more unrealistic and dogmatic thoughts than do less upset individuals.

This widespread interest in irrational ideas has had some bad as well as good results. For humans create many kinds—perhaps hundreds—of irrationalities, which tend to influence their feelings and make them act inefficiently. But not all of these irrationalities, by any means, lead to neurosis.

If you believe that you are a good poker player when you really are not, you will probably foolishly risk playing with good players—and will often lose. If, however, you irrationally believe that you *must* be a great poker player and that you *have to* continually show others how good you are, you then probably will compulsively gamble and keep gambling even when you steadily lose.

After I described the first twelve basic iBs of REBT in 1956, I continued to explore my clients' irrationalities. To my surprise, I discovered that I could condense my original list into three main iBs—and that these were all *musts* instead of *preferences*. The three basic *musts* that create emotional problems are:

1. "*I* must perform well and/or win the approval of important people or else *I* am an *inadequate person!*"
2. "*You* must treat me fairly and considerately and not unduly frustrate me or else *you* are a rotten individual."
3. "My life conditions *must* give me the things I want and *have to* have to keep me from harm or else *life* is unbearable and I *can't* be happy at all!"

As I boiled down the previous irrational ideas I had discovered into these three major *musts*, I also found that my clients' other up-setting beliefs were not independent but were consciously or unconsciously derived from their musts.

Take, for example, one of the most popular iBs, which I have named *awfulizing* or *horribleizing:* "It's *awful* if I fail at this important task and it's *horrible* if people reject me for failing."

This is a crazy idea because although it may be highly *unfortunate* for you to fail and very *inconvenient* for you to be rejected, when you call failure and rejection *awful* and *horrible* you imply that they are *more than* bad or 101 percent inconvenient—which, of course, they cannot be. They aren't even 100 percent bad—because they could usually be *worse.* When you overgeneralize and go *beyond* reality in this way, you will make yourself feel panicked and depressed (instead of appropriately sorry and frustrated) if you fail and get rejected.

Now *why* does a bright person like you resort to this kind of silly, unrealistic awfulizing? Mainly, I contend, because you start with a conscious or unconscious *must* and *then* you easily and "logically" derive your awfulizing from it. Thus, you start with "I absolutely *must* perform this task well!" Then you "reasonably" conclude, "And since I didn't perform as well as I absolutely *must*, it's *awful*, it's *more than* inconvenient, it's as bad *as it possibly could be*, it's the *end of the world!*"

If you *only* stayed with your *preference* for doing well and *never* escalated it into a *dire necessity*, a *must*, would you awfulize about your poor performance? Hardly ever! I contend. For your preference statement would be, "I would *like to* perform this task well, but I don't ever *have to*. So if I fail, too bad—but not awful!"

Take another set of iBs: personalizing and all-or-none thinking: "Now that the person I truly love has rejected me, I'm sure I *acted very badly*. Therefore, I am a thoroughly *inadequate person* who will *always* be rejected and *never* be loved by someone for whom I care."

These ideas are irrational and self-defeating because:

1. You may not have acted badly at all and still may have been rejected because the person you love has unique tastes or prejudices. In fact, you may act so well that your beloved may conclude that you are *too good* and that therefore he or she had better reject you before you later do the rejecting.
2. Even if you act badly with your beloved and therefore get rejected, you are hardly an *inadequate* person but a *person who* acted inadequately *this time* and who can learn to act better in the future.
3. Just because you get rejected now doesn't prove that you'll *always* be rejected and *never* be accepted by everyone for whom you care. If you keep trying, that's most improbable. Your conclusion is a silly overgeneralization.

Now why, again, does a reasonable person like you make such crazy conclusions?

Not because you simply *want* to be accepted. For then you would conclude that it's undesirable when you are rejected and would keep trying for future approval. You might possibly criticize your *efforts* but hardly damn *yourself* when a loved one rejects you.

But suppose you irrationally begin with strong and devout *musts*—such as, "I *must* win the love of everyone I truly love and must *never* be rejected!" You will then *easily* and *naturally* conclude, "Because I have been rejected, as I *must* not be, I am sure I acted badly and am an *inadequate person* who will *never* be loved the way I *must* be!"

REBT, then, shows how you upset yourself with absolutistic shoulds, oughts, and musts. It holds that you can nicely hold *condi-*

tional and *logical* musts—such as, "If I want to read this book, I must buy or borrow a copy." And: "If I want to get a degree at college, I must get passing marks in my required subjects." For these conventional musts merely say, "*If* I want something, then I *have to* act properly to get it." This kind of *must* is (though not always) realistic and helps you to act sensibly.

REBT accepts your realistic *musts* but shows you how to look for your *un*conditional and *il*logical musts. Such as: "Even if I can't get a copy of this book, I still *must* read it." And: "Although I have not passed any college courses, because I strongly want a degree they *should* give it to me!"

REBT adds this rule to Insight No. 3: In seeking to discover the irrational Beliefs (iBs) you use to disturb yourself, *cherchez le* should, *cherchez le* must! *Look for your dogmatic shoulds and musts!*

Using REBT, you can quickly find these musts and see how you needlessly upset yourself by devoutly holding them. If you look!

Sandra insisted that she first felt that being rejected by a lover was *awful* and *terrible*, and that once she felt that way, she *then* said that she *must* not get rejected. To begin with, she insisted, she only had strong *desires*, and not *demands*, to be loved.

I was quite skeptical. "Let's suppose," I said, "you *only* wanted your lover strongly, and were not *also* insisting that you *must* not lose him. What would your entire belief be about having and losing him?"

"Uh—. I guess, I strongly *want* him to love me. And if he doesn't, that's *terrible* and I *can't stand it!*"

"You're implying that if you only *weakly* wanted him to love you and if he didn't, that would be somewhat *inconvenient* but hardly terrible. Right?"

"Yes, only when I see that my strong desire for him may be blocked do I feel that it's terrible."

"But suppose you believed, 'I strongly *want* my lover to love me but he really doesn't *have to*. I really don't *need* him to love me, though I truly *desire* him to do so.' How would you *then* feel if you lost him?"

"Well—uh— If I really believed he didn't *have to* love me, that I don't *need* him to, I guess I would feel that I could go on without him and it wouldn't be so terrible. But it would be quite frustrating and bad."

"See! If you were not making his loving you a *necessity* but only a *strong desire*, you would feel highly *frustrated* and *inconvenienced*. The stronger your desire for his love is, the *more* inconvenienced you will be. But to turn your great inconvenience into a *holy horror*, to make it *terrible*, you are really adding a second idea: 'Since losing my lover is *so* bad, I *must* not be *that* inconvenienced. And if I am so *very* frustrated, as I *must* not be, that is *awful*, that is terrible!' "

"So my *awfulizing* about losing my lover really stems from my *musturbating* about such a *great* loss?"

"Doesn't it? If you *only* stayed with a preference sentence, wouldn't you be saying to yourself, 'I hate like hell losing my lover. But there is still no reason why I *must* not lose him'?"

"Yes, I guess I would."

"And would you not then conclude, 'Because there is no reason why I *must* not lose him, it would be highly obnoxious if I did, but the world won't come to an end, it won't be *terrible*, and I could still be a happy—though a less happy—person'?"

"Yes, I might well conclude that."

"I think you would! Your *awfulizing* and *terribleizing* basically stems from your *command, your necessity*, that this very bad loss *must* not occur."

"If I tell myself, 'Losing him is *awful*!' am I then saying that this loss *must* not exist?"

"Not always. You may just be using *awful* when you really mean, 'It's *very bad* losing him,' and that would merely make you feel healthily sad and frustrated at this loss. But when you say to yourself, 'It's awful *that* I lost him,' you may also mean, 'It's *more than* bad, it *must not be* that bad, I *can't bear* that degree of badness!' Your *must* is crucial here. For missing out on your strong desire to be loved may indeed be *very* bad and may help you feel *quite* sorrowful. But telling yourself that this degree of badness *absolutely ought not* exist and therefore is *more than* bad puts you outside of reality and makes you severely anxious and depressed. Do you see the difference?"

"I think I do. But it's hard to see it clearly and keep seeing it."

"True! Moreover, once you say to yourself, 'I *must* not lose my lover, and it would be *terrible* if I did,' you then tend to add, in a circular fashion, 'And since it would be so *terrible*, this loss *must not* occur, absolutely *should not* exist!' And then you foolishly think that your *musts* stem from your *terribleizing*."

"When only the *second* must does! Is that what you mean?"

"Yes. You *bring musts or demands* to the possible loss of your lover. You therefore define this loss as *terrible*. Then you *bring* the demand that 'terrible things *must* not exist!' to your terribleizing. So you have first-level and second-level *musts* that you tend to bring to undesirable situations. And you therefore have, very often, primary and secondary disturbances."

"Both of which I *make* exist because I tell myself that bad and 'horrible' things *must* not happen to me."

"Yes, that's a good point you're making. You can think that mildly bad, very bad, and so-called terrible events *must* not occur. And in all these cases, even with the mildly bad events, you'll needlessly disturb yourself. While if you convince yourself that even if the very worst things in life—such as painful deaths—*should* and *must* at times exist, because they simply and truly *do* exist, then you'll tend to feel sad and frustrated, but *not* severely anxious and depressed."

"I see now that the *must* seems to be basic to my disturbances," said Sandra.

"Fine. But don't let me talk you into this. Figure it out for yourself. Whenever you really feel miserable—especially panicked, depressed, or enraged—look for your *should*, look for your *must*. And then see that if you gave it up, you'll still feel frustrated and saddened—but not off the wall!"

"Okay, I'll really keep looking."

Sandra did keep looking for her *musts* and *shoulds*—as well as for the *awfulizing* and *terribleizing* that stemmed from them—and for the first time in her life managed to feel quite sad but not depressed when an important lover rejected her. When she occasionally sank into depression again, she saw she had returned to *must*urbation, worked at giving it up, and then felt alone and sad but not self-downing or depressed.

It is about time that I fully explain some confusing aspects of your Belief system. This system includes rational Beliefs (rBs) and preferences (which are also rational), which also includes irrational Beliefs (iBs) and absolutistic shoulds, oughts, and musts (which are also irrational).

I was wise enough to pioneeringly point out in my first paper on REBT at the American Psychological Association convention in Chicago in 1956 that Beliefs include thinking, feeling, and behaving—all three processes. Feelings also include thinking and behavings; and behavings also include thinking and feeling. Again, all three.

However, in some of my early writings, I carelessly used the term "Beliefs" as if it included only thinking; I omitted saying that Beliefs are full of feeling and of actions, *too*. I later corrected this in my books, as in *Feeling Better, Getting Better, and Staying Better*, in *Overcoming Destructive Beliefs, Feelings, and Behaviors*, and in other recent writings. I did not make this correction in the first edition of the present book and wish to make it quite clear now.

My original ABCs of REBT are still accurate if, by B, Belief System, you (and I!) clearly understand that Beliefs include, influence, and are integrally related to feelings and actions. When you think about something, you really THINK-feel-and act about it. When you feel about something, you really FEEL-think-and act about it. When you act about something, you really ACT-think-and feel about it. That is your nature—both innate and learned; and unless you are brain injured or otherwise defective, you think-feel-act. So when I use *Belief* and *Belief System* in this book, try to realize—which is difficult—that I really mean think-feel-and-act. That is why REBT, as I shall show, has so many important emotional and behavioral methods, in addition to its cognitive methods, to help you change your dysfunctional thinking-feeling-behaving.

I particularly bring that to your attention again on page 85.

REBT Exercise No. 7

Look for something that you really believe is *awful, terrible*, or *horrible*. See if you can find—as you most probably can—the *must* that lurks behind your defining this thing or act as *awful*.

Example: "I think that being rejected by a person I truly love is *awful*."

Hidden musts

". . . Because I *must* not be rejected by anyone I truly love."

". . . Because I *must* be good enough to win the favor of anyone I truly love."

". . . Because I *must* not be deprived of the companionship of someone I really love."

". . . Because I am a nice person who *deserves* to be loved, and therefore the world *must* arrange things so that I get the love I truly deserve!"

Look for something you think you *can't stand* and try to discover some of the *musts* that make you feel that you *can't stand* this thing.

Example: "The conditions under which I work are so disorganized and unfair that I *can't stand* working there."

Hidden musts

"The conditions under which I work are *so* disorganized and unfair that they *must not* exist. And therefore I *can't stand* their being as bad as they *must* not be."

"I *must* have pleasure and relaxation at work, and I cannot have this when the conditions there are so disorganized and unfair. Therefore, these conditions are so bad that I *can't stand* them."

"I *must* have *some degree* of happiness at work, and the conditions there are so disorganized and unfair that I can't be happy *at all* there. Therefore, I *can't stand* working there."

"My work *must* be the way I want it to be, and the disorganized and unfair conditions where I work don't allow this. Therefore, I *can't stand* working there."

Look for some occasion when you felt you were an inadequate

person, or felt worthless, or felt undeserving of good things. Try to discover your hidden musts that made you feel this way.

Example: "I failed a good many times to establish a long-term relationship with someone for whom I really cared. That shows what an inadequate, unlovable person I am."

Hidden musts

"I *must* succeed in at least one long-term relationship, otherwise I am an inadequate, unlovable person."

"I *must* not *keep* failing at relationships with people for whom I care, and if I do I am clearly worthless."

"Because having a good relationship is the most important thing for me, I *have to* achieve one soon. If I fail at this, as I *must* not, I am obviously an inferior, undeserving person."

"I am *sometimes* allowed to fail at long-term relationships, but I have failed *too many* times, as I *must* not! Failing so *many times* shows that I am an inadequate, unlovable person!"

Look for some time when you felt hopeless and knew you would *never* succeed in life and would *always* be deprived of what you most wanted. Find your hidden musts that led you to this feeling of hopelessness.

Example: "Now that I have lost several good jobs, I'll *never* be able to get and keep a good one and *always* will be doomed to a lousy position."

Hidden musts

"I *must* never keep losing good jobs, and if I do, I'll clearly *never* be able to get and keep a good one."

"I *have to* stay on a good job for a reasonable length of time. Otherwise, I'll *never* be able to get another good one and *always* be doomed to poor ones."

"I *must* prove what a worthwhile worker and person I am and will never be worthwhile if I keep losing good jobs. Being worthless, I'll never be able to get and keep a good job!"

"I can lose a good job now and then but *must* not keep losing so many of them. Since I keep losing them, as I *must* not, I'll *never* be able to keep a good one and *always* will be doomed to a lousy position."

Whenever you are upset about anything, look for your obvious or hidden dogmatic *musts*. Assume that you really have them; and if you can't find them ask a friend, relative, or therapist to help you look for them. *Cherchez le* should, *cherchez le* must. Seek and ye shall find!

9

REBT Insight No. 4: Forget Your "Godawful" Past!

For several years I was a highly successful psychoanalyst and thought that I was greatly helping my clients by exploring the gory details of their early life and showing them how these experiences made them disturbed—and how they could not understand and remove these early influences. How wrong I was!

After I honestly admitted that my psychoanalytic "cures" were hardly as good as I would have liked them to be, I began to see that helping people to understand their past was not only doing them little good but was actually blocking their dealing with their *preset* problems. So I founded REBT and began to help my clients in the present and to help them with their current difficulties. I immediately experienced better results in teaching them how to be "unneurotic."

Many of my clients, however, still insisted on talking about their past—partly because they previously had years of psychoanalysis and had been trained to do so. I then showed them that, yes, their mother or brother had severely criticized them during their childhood (at point A, or Activating Event, in the ABCs of REBT). And, yes, they had then undoubtedly felt depressed and self-downing (at point C, or Consequence). But A did *not* cause or create (though it may well have contributed to) C.

B (their Belief System) was the main contributor to C; and B included a rational Belief (rB)—such as, "I don't like being criticized. Maybe it shows that I'm doing something wrong and, if so, I'd better correct it." But B also included an irrational Belief (iB) and a dysfunctional feeling, such as, "I *need* my mother's love and absolutely *must not* act badly and get her disapproval. If she, whom I *need*, dislikes me, I am surely an unlovable, crummy person!"

So I showed my early REBT clients the iBs and dysfunctional feelings that they *brought* to their early childhood situations. I proved to them that, as children, they basically *upset themselves.*

More important, I demonstrated by examining their present lives how they were *still* using these same early iBs to castigate themselves and that they were *therefore* currently disturbed. Unlike many other people who were upset during childhood but long since *changed* their thinking and got over downing themselves (and hating their parents), these clients still actively *clung* to their original shoulds and musts and refused to give them up.

Their early thoughts and feelings did not *make them* anxious today. Rather, their *present* and *continuing* dogmas and feelings (iBs) were really the more direct cause of their current neurosis.

This brings us to Insight No. 4 of REBT: *Your early childhood experiences and your past conditioning did not originally make you disturbed. You did.*

You chose, because of your disturbed thinking and feelings, to overreact or underreact to the Activating Events and Experiences of the past. You were actually an integral *part* of these Experiences.

Because when you do something (say, take a boat trip), you approach the situation (the boat, the people on it, the water on which it sails), and you *react*, as only *you* can react, to it. Moreover, you bring your memories of past events (including your reactions to these events) to the new situation, and you therefore "experience" it in a biased manner. You largely (though not completely) *are* your experiences—are an active creator of them.

So to some extent you "invented" your past. And when "it" supposedly "makes you" feel upset today, you are really choosing to keep it alive. How?

1. By thinking the same kind of irrational Beliefs (iBs) with which you upset yourself—during your childhood. For example, "I not only *want* my mother's approval but I completely *need* it and am a *basket case* without it!"
2. By still actively *holding on to* these views and feelings today.
3. By refusing to rethink and act against your iBs until you no longer use them to upset yourself.

In the past, you largely *made* your bed of neurosis and you are *insisting* on lying in it today! If, therefore, you use REBT to understand your early life, you can focus on *your* part in creating it and on how *you* now perpetuate your childish thoughts, feelings, and behaviors.

Ironically, if you forget about your past, if you assume that you are still bothering yourself *today*, and if you look for what you are *now* doing to make yourself miserable, you will often see what *really* "happened" in your childhood—and what you did to *make it happen*. The less you gripe about your past, the more you tend to admit that you partly created it. The more you explore what you are *now* doing to cause your upset feelings, the more insight you will have.

Karen, a member of one of my regular therapy groups at the Albert Ellis Institute in New York, kept insisting that she hated herself because all during her childhood her mother continually told her that she was stupid and ugly. Rob, another group member, backed her up by stoutly contending that he had no confidence in himself because his father insisted that he become a wealthy businessman, and he actually turned out to be a low-paid civil servant.

The other group members and I tried to show Karen and Rob that their brothers and sisters, who had also been severely put down by their parents, were—peculiarly enough!—confident and self-accepting. No sale. Karen and Rob firmly held on to their "traumatic" pasts—and did little to change themselves in the present.

Audrey, an attractive dentist, who had loathed herself all her life and was still shy and unassertive, finally spoke up: "I'm sick and tired of the two of you moaning and wailing about your goddamned parents and how they made you the way you are. Let me tell you about my mother and father. They were the nicest and most gentle people I ever met. They loved me and supported me in every which way. They always told me I was bright and beautiful and that they knew I could do anything I wanted to do. They treated my brother equally well; and he was, and still is, very kind to me. Well, as a result of all this marvelous upbringing, you know what a basket case I now am—as meek and self-hating as I possibly could be! So why don't both of you stop your shrieking about your horrible childhood and get on with your *present* lives? Just as I have to do about mine—in spite of my wonderful upbringing!"

Three other members of the group joined Audrey in affirming that they, too, had had fine, loving parents—and still hated themselves. One of them, Jose, said, "I now see, through REBT, that I brought my perfectionistic *self* to my tolerant mother and father. No matter how often *they* accepted me, *I* pigheadedly refused to do so. And I *still* refuse! So I keep working to change *me* and *my* perfectionism. As you two had better do also!"

Surprised by the group's reaction, Karen and Rob were taken aback. Karen did some more thinking, worked hard at accepting herself with her failings, and then was able to forgive her mother and have a good relationship with her. Rob temporarily stopped resenting his father but then went back to blaming him again for all his present problems. He quit the group, was in psychoanalysis for the past five years, and according to one of his friends who regularly attended my Friday night workshops, continued to spend most of his therapy sessions angrily damning his father.

Too bad. But REBT can't win them all. And obviously doesn't!

REBT Exercise No. 8

Try to remember an event from your early life when you felt horrified, depressed, or self-hating. Then, see if you can figure out your rational Beliefs (rBs) and irrational Beliefs (iBs) that you held at that time that probably led you to feeling emotionally upset. See how you hold on to them today.

Example: "My parents often made me wear ill-fitting hand-me-down clothes, and I felt so ashamed that I often stayed at home and refused to play with the other kids."

Rational beliefs (rBs): "I don't like wearing ill-fitting clothes and possibly being laughed at by the other kids. But I can bear it and still get along with the kids who may laugh at me."

Early irrational beliefs (iBs): "I *must* not wear these ill-fitting clothes and be laughed at by the other kids. How awful and shameful. They must think I'm a fool—and they're right, I am!"

Present irrational beliefs (iBs): "I make sure I don't wear ill-fitting clothes today. But I still think that if anyone laughs at me and thinks I'm a fool I agree that I am and feel very ashamed."

Example: "My teachers treated me uncaringly and unfairly when I was a child, and that made me very angry and rebellious."

Rational beliefs (rBs): "I wish my teachers would treat me caringly and fairly, and it is most unfortunate that they don't. But that is their poor behavior, and they are not totally rotten people for acting that way."

Early irrational beliefs (iBs): "My parents *absolutely should* treat me caringly and fairly, and it is awful that they don't. They are thoroughly rotten people for acting in that horrible way, and I hope they drop dead!"

Present irrational beliefs (iBs): "Some people still treat me uncaringly and unfairly today—and they *absolutely should not!* These people are thoroughly rotten people, and I hope they get severely punished!"

Whenever you think that your early experiences have made you or conditioned you to be disturbed today, recall and relive these experiences and figure out your rational Beliefs (rBs) and especially your irrational Beliefs (iBs) that mainly led to your past emotional problems, and also see how you are still clinging to these iBs today.

10

REBT Insight No. 5: Actively Dispute Your Irrational Beliefs

So you are now beginning to have insight into your irrational Beliefs—especially into your dogmatic shoulds and musts. Great!

But you won't do yourself much good, nor will you remove your neurotic misery, unless you actively and forcefully dispute your iBs.

Understanding is not enough, any more than understanding how to drive a car will make you a good driver. What are you going to *do* about knowing the ABCs of REBT and about the irrational Beliefs that you use to keep yourself disturbed?

At the time I write this, I have twenty or more clients who are well aware of their iBs but who are doing little to dispute them. Irene has been in one of my therapy groups for four months; she often helps other members by pointing out their irrationalities and vigorously showing them that there is no reason why they must be in a good relationship or have to marry. But she thinks that because she is approaching thirty-five and has never had a long-term relationship, she absolutely *must* marry very soon.

Irene keeps telling the group, "I think it would be desirable if I marry but I don't *have to*." She then secretly sneaks in, "But I really *must*!" And she rarely challenges and rips up her own *must*—so she remains quite anxious.

Frank, another member of Irene's therapy group, shows Irene her musts but tries to give her only practical solutions about her need to marry soon—like suggesting good places for her to meet suitable males. In his own case, he does the same thing: He looks for "good" ways to argue with his obnoxious boss instead of giving up his own demand that his boss *must* not be obnoxious.

Josie, a third member of this group, keeps insisting that because Irene *is* getting older and because she dotes on children, she really *should* find a husband soon. Needless to say, Josie is hardly helping herself give up her own demands—that her daughter and her husband *must* be caring and fair to her—and she definitely is not helping Irene.

So REBT includes Insight No. 5: *Fully acknowledge that you upset yourself with irrational musts. Acknowledging that you have musts will not in itself make them disappear. Fight them in many ways that REBT provides, but above all actively challenge and dispute them.*

When you are irrational, you oppose reason (good sense) and refuse to accept reality (the way things are). Science tells you how to use reason, logic, and facts to surrender your irrational thinking. It raises skeptical questions:

- "Where is the evidence that I *must* succeed?"
- "Why do people *have to* treat me fairly?"
- "Where is it written that my life has *got to be* free of hassles?"

When you use scientific questioning and disputing you figure out answers like these:

- "There is no evidence that I *must* succeed, though I would very much prefer to do so."
- "People *don't* have to treat me fairly, although it would be lovely if they did!"
- "My life never *has to be* free of major hassles and probably never will be. But I can still lead an enjoyable existence! And I can even learn and benefit from the hassles!"

Is REBT a self-treatment method that specializes in arguing and persuading? It is. With a vengeance! It holds that disputing, disputing, and disputing irrational Beliefs is one of the most important means of overcoming your emotional problems.

Let us go back to the ABCs of REBT and proceed to D, Disputing. How would you Dispute if you had the problem presented in chapter 5? Let us see.

G (Your goal)—you want a good job.

A (Your activating event)—you do badly in an interview and fail to get the job you desire.

rBs (Your rational beliefs)—"I don't like failing to get this job! How frustrating! Too bad! How can I try to do better next time?"

iBs (Your irrational beliefs)—"No matter what, I *must* get this interviewer to like me and give me this job! If he doesn't, it's *awful*! I can't stand it! If I fail, that proves that I'm an incompetent person who will never be able to get and keep a good position."

C (Consequence of holding your irrational beliefs)—you feel depressed and worthless. You avoid going for other interviews.

Now that we have outlined the ABCs about your Goal of getting a good job, let us proceed to D—to scientifically Dispute your irrational Beliefs (iBs):

iB—"No matter what, I *must* get this interviewer to like me and give me this job."

D (disputing)—"Why *must* I get this interviewer to like me? Where is the evidence that he *has to* give me this job?"

E (effective new philosophy)—"There is no reason why I *must* get this interviewer to like me, though there are several reasons why I would *prefer* that. No evidence exists that he *has to* give me this job. If the universe ruled that he *had to* give it to me, he obviously would. But it doesn't. Too bad!"

iB—If I don't get this job, as I *must*, it's *awful*!"

D (disputing)—"In what way is it *awful* if I don't get this job?"

E (effective new philosophy)—"In no way. It may be damned inconvenient. But it is hardly 100 percent inconvenient, since it could be worse. And if it were *awful* or *terrible* it would be *more than* (101 percent) inconvenient—which, of course, it can't be. So it's very inconvenient! Tough!"

iB—"If I don't get this job, as I *must*, I can't stand it."

D (disputing)—"Prove that I can't stand it."

E (effective new philosophy)—"I can't prove that because I obviously *can* stand it. First of all, I will hardly die if I lose this job. Second, if I really couldn't *stand* it, I couldn't be happy at *all* without this job. But clearly there are many ways in which I can be happy, even if I never get as good a job as this one."

iB—"My losing this job proves that I'm an incompetent person who will never be able to get and keep a good position."

D (disputing)—"Where is this written?"

E (effective new philosophy)—"Only in my nutty head! If I lose this job it may not at all show that I am incompetent—but only that this particular interviewer didn't like me. And even if I acted incompetently to the interviewer, that only indicates that I am a *person who acted badly this time* and not a totally *incompetent person*. Even if I often am incompetent at interviews, that doesn't prove that I will *never* be able to get and keep a good position. So I'd better start looking again!"

If you keep actively and vigorously Disputing your irrational Beliefs—at point D in REBT—you scientifically challenge them until you prove them wrong and give them up. And you change C—in this case, your depression and self-denigration. If you keep strongly Disputing your iBs, your disturbed Consequences rarely return.

As you give up your unhealthy feelings of depression and wormhood, you also are able to change your behavior and can keep going fairly easily on more interviews and continue looking for a job.

To return to Irene, the member of my therapy group mentioned above, she finally admitted that, on the one hand, she was telling herself, "I don't *have to* marry" but, on the other hand, she was even more strongly convincing herself, "But I really *must*." She and the other group members then kept vigorously Disputing her irrational *must* until she finally got to—and really believed—the bottom line:

"It is indeed highly desirable if I marry. But if I never find a suitable mate, I can *still* be a happy person. I *can*! And will! No matter what!"

After weeks of accepting this new Effective Rational Philosophy (E), Irene's panic vanished, even though her strong desires and goals to marry remained. She then felt healthily *disappointed* but not *depressed* about still being single.

Frank, doing some amount of active Disputing but not as much as Irene, partially gave up the irrational Belief that his boss *must* not act obnoxiously, but he from time to time returned to it. Josie at first refused to surrender her demands that her daughter and her husband *must* be caring and fair to her. But when she saw how Irene overcame her panic about being single, she was able to accept, though not like, her uncaring family. As she noted to the group: "Dammit, they just *are* the way they are. And I didn't *make* them that way. They have their own fine talents at being cold and unloving. Why should they *not* behave badly—when they obviously *do*!" Believing and feeling this, Josie became less obsessed with her family and more devoted to Chinese art—which rarely treated her unjustly!

REBT Exercise No. 9

Find something that you are now or have recently been emotionally upset about or that you acted foolishly about. Write it down.

For example:

- Someone lied to you and you felt furious and homicidal.
- You failed to do your regular exercises and you felt angry at yourself and very depressed.
- You wore an informal outfit to a formal affair and felt highly embarrassed or ashamed.
- You were severely criticized by a friend you had helped, and you felt extremely hurt and self-pitying.
- You promised yourself to stop smoking and didn't stop.
- You selfishly harmed an innocent person.
- You gave into a plane phobia—drove a thousand miles to get somewhere.

• You put yourself down for not overcoming one of your phobias or compulsions.

When you remember the present or past time that you felt disturbed or acted self-defeatingly, assume that you had an irrational should, ought, or must and look for it.

Example: "The person who lied to me absolutely should not have done that! How terrible that she acted the way she *must* not act!"

Also look for the common irrational Beliefs that often accompany your *musts*. Write them down:

Awfulizing, horribleizing, terribleizing
Example: "Since I acted so stupidly about wearing that informal outfit to a formal affair, as I clearly *should* not have done, that's *terrible*! It's *awful* that I can't dress properly."

"I can't-stand-it-itis"
Example: "When friends whom I have helped and supported severely criticize me, as they definitely *should* not, I *can't stand it!* I *can't bear* such ingratitude!"

Feelings of worthlessness and self-hatred
Example: "Because I didn't follow my promise to stop smoking, as I *should* have done, I'm a *stupid, worthless person.* Considering how important it is to stop, I'm really *no good* for continuing to smoke."

Feelings of undeservingness and self-damnation
Example: "Because I selfishly harmed my innocent friend, as I *absolutely should not* have done, I am a *damnable person* who *deserves to be punished.* I am *undeserving* of any acceptance by others and should be severely boycotted."

Belief in allness, neverness, and totality
Example: "Now that I have stupidly given in to my plane phobia and driven a thousand miles to get from New York to Chicago, as I definitely *should not* have done, I'll *never* be able to overcome my irrational fear of planes, I'll *always* have to drive instead of fly long distances, and I am *totally* unable to conquer my phobia."

Belief in perfection, specialness, and grandiosity
Example: "I must be perfect, special, and noble and if I am less

than this, I am not really a good or worthy person. If I am not super-special, I am nothing!"

Now actively Dispute (at point D) your irrational Beliefs (iBs) by asking scientific questions about them and assuming that if you keep questioning and challenging them you can definitely change them to preferences or give them up entirely. Here are some of the main Disputing questions you can ask:

Disputing question: "Why is my iB true? Why does it not conform to reality?"

Example: "Why *shouldn't* people who lie to me do what they do—lie? Why *must* not they act in that way and why is it *terrible* if they do?"

Answer: There is no reason why they *should not* or *must* not lie, though it would be highly desirable if they didn't. Actually, if they are prone to lying right now, they *must* keep lying—for that is their nature. And if they do lie, it is hardly *terrible* (or badder than it *should* be) but only highly inconvenient. And I can live with that inconvenience."

Disputing question: "Where is the evidence that my irrational Beliefs (iBs) are true? Where are the facts to sustain them?"

Example: "Where is the evidence that I should not have acted stupidly and worn that informal outfit to a formal affair? Where are the facts to prove that it's *terrible* that I did so?"

Answer: "There is no evidence that I *should not* have acted so stupidly, and there is considerable evidence that I am a fallible human who consequently will at times behave quite stupidly. There are no facts to prove that it's *terrible* that I did this, but only facts to show that I encouraged some people to think less of my behavior (and probably of me) and that's unfortunate, but I can still win the approval of many people and lead a good life."

Disputing question: "Where is it written that my irrational Beliefs (iBs) are true? Who says that they exist in reality?"

Example: "Where is it written that friends I have helped *absolutely should not* criticize me severely and that I *can't stand it* when they do? Who says that I *can't bear* such severe criticism?"

Answer: "It is only written in my head that they *must not* criticize me, since obviously they are not heeding my command. I *can* stand it when they do severely criticize me because their words can't hurt me unless *I* sharpen them and take them too seriously. Since I won't die from their criticism and can still accept myself in spite of it, I *can* bear it—and perhaps even benefit from heeding some of it."

Disputing question: "In what way can I support these irrational Beliefs (iBs)? How can I prove their validity?"

Example: "In what way am I a *stupid, worthless person* because I didn't follow my promise to stop smoking, as I *should* have followed it? How does this stupid act of smoking make me *no good*?"

Answer: "In no way am I, a total person, *stupid and worthless* because I keep doing a stupid act like smoking. My *act* is foolish but that hardly makes me a *worthless* fool, only a *person who* is now acting foolishly, who may act less foolishly in the future, and who does many other intelligent things. *It*, this stupid act of smoking, is no good (or of little good) but *I* am not *it*. I am I, and I have the ability to do many good things and many bad acts. I also have the ability to change my bad deeds for good ones. So let me see how I can now stop smoking!"

Disputing question: "Is there any way in which I can falsify or invalidate my irrational Beliefs (iBs)?"

Example: "Is there any way in which I can falsify or invalidate my Belief that because I selfishly harmed my innocent friend, as I absolutely should not, I am a *damnable person* who *deserves* to be punished? Can I really prove or disprove the idea that I am undeserving of any acceptance by others and should be severely boycotted and punished?"

Answer: "No, I cannot falsify my belief that I am a *damnable person* who *deserves* to be punished. I can prove that I selfishly harmed my innocent friend, which was wrong. But I can only arbitrarily insist that the wrongness or evil makes me a *damnable, undeserving person* who absolutely *should be* punished and deprived of all human acceptance and pleasure.

Concepts like damnation, undeservingness, and total unacceptability as a human imply that there is some superhuman higher power that absolutely knows when human acts are bad enough to levy such undebatable sanctions. But such superhuman powers cannot be proved or disproved, so there is no way to falsify (or to verify) these exceptionally punitive concepts. To believe in them leads to extreme self-damnation and self-deprivation. But since I cannot justify or falsify these irrational Beliefs, and they are therefore matters of pure choice, why should I choose to self-defeatingly believe them? For no good reason!"

Disputing question: "What results will I get if I continue to hold these irrational Beliefs? What good—and harm—will it bring me to believe them?"

Example: "What results will I get if I believe that I *absolutely should not* have given in to my plane phobia and driven a thousand miles to get from New York to Chicago, and that therefore I'll *never* be able to overcome my irrational fear of planes? What results will I achieve if I firmly believe that I'll *always* have to drive instead of fly long distances?"

Answer: "Very poor results! If I rigidly hold to this overgeneralized way of thinking, I will doom myself to my all-and-never predictions and *make* my phobia a hopeless condition. Whenever I insist that I *can't* change and that I must *always* function badly, I block my progress and practically force myself to stick in the mud."

Disputing question: "Can I choose to stop believing and following my irrational Beliefs?"

Example: "Can I choose to believe that I do not have to be perfect, special, and noble and choose to give up the belief that if I am not all I am nothing?"

Answer: "Of course I can! Anything I choose to believe I can obviously choose not to believe. Even if I am strongly indoctrinated—or indoctrinate myself—with these nutty beliefs in my early life, I may have to make some effort to change them, but as long as they are *my* ideas I can choose to change them or give them up. Many of the things I once believed I no longer hold to, and any notion I now choose to cling to I can later change. So let me work at changing my irrational and self-defeating Beliefs to those that will bring me better results!"

Once you have written down some of your dogmatic *musts* and the other irrational Beliefs (iBs) that they tend to lead to, ask yourself the Disputing questions listed above and do your best to answer them until you at least temporarily change these Beliefs to rational preferences. Do this until you feel much better and have changed your unhealthy feelings and behaviors for more appropriate ones. Repeat this exercise whenever you feel quite disturbed or act in a distinctly self-defeating manner. If necessary, repeat it two, three, or more times a day when you feel seriously anxious, depressed, hostile, self-hating, or self-pitying.

11

REBT Insight No. 6: You Can Refuse to Upset Yourself About Upsetting Yourself

Many therapies, such as behavior therapy, try to relieve people's neurotic symptoms—their phobias, obsessions, compulsions, and addictions. Some therapies, such as existential analysis and psychoanalysis, try to go "deeper" and help clients change their philosophy, and thus prevent them from creating new symptoms in the future. REBT goes still further and aims for a profound new philosophy as well as for relieving symptoms. It also helps people become unanxious and undepressed *about* their neurotic problems.

REBT's view that crooked thinking leads to emotional problems has much evidence to support it, as I have already noted. But it is also supported by the very nature of neurosis. As I point out in *Reason and Emotion in Psychotherapy* and *A Guide to Rational Living*, we may drive rats and guinea pigs "neurotic" in psychological laboratories, but they do not seem to *know* they are disturbed. They don't *observe* their crazy behavior, or *think* about it, or *hate themselves* for suffering from it. Humans often do.

People continually *see* that they are anxious, *know* that worry is inefficient, *measure* how bad it is, *accept responsibility* for producing it, and *criticize* themselves for "weakly" or "stupidly" bringing it on. They then tend to make themselves anxious about their anxiety, depressed about their depression, guilty about their addictions, self-pitying about their neurosis.

George is often angry at his senile, demanding mother—and hates himself intensely for being angry at her. Cynthia smokes two packs of cigarettes a day in spite of her weak lungs and steady coughing and is very guilty about her "horrible weakness." Josef is unassertive with his woman-friend—and angry at her for "making him" afraid to assert himself.

Are disturbances about disturbances important? Indeed they are! For if George hates himself for being angry at his mother, he will tend to be so wrapped up in his self-denigration that he will have little time and energy to work on the problem of giving up his anger. If Cynthia is guilty about her "horrible weakness" of continuing to smoke when she has weak lungs, she will upset herself so severely that she may "need" more cigarettes to distract her from her self-hatred. While Josef remains angry at his woman-friend for "making" him unassertive, he will be aggressive rather than assertive and will hardly work on expressing himself. By bringing on their disturbances *about* their original neuroses, George, Cynthia, and Josef will *add* considerably to their emotional problems.

This brings us to Insight No. 6 of REBT: *Once you make yourself miserable about anything, you easily tend to make yourself miserable about your misery. If you look at what you are doing, you can often discover that you are making yourself anxious about your anxiety, depressed about your depression, and guilty about your rage. You really are talented at upsetting yourself!*

Don't take my word for it. Be honest with yourself. How did you really feel when you were last panicked? Yes, how did you feel *about* your panic? And *about* your last bout of depression? And *about* your severe feelings of inadequacy? See!

The REBT solution? Oddly enough, more thinking, more reasoning. When you create problems *about* problems by *observing* your bad feelings and *telling yourself* that you *must not* have these feelings, you can remove them by using Insight No. 6.

To be more precise, to stop disturbing yourself about disturbing yourself, try the following steps:

1. *Ask yourself,* "Now that I feel very anxious, am I *also* anxious *about* my anxiety?"
2. *Acknowledge,* when you find them, your secondary symptoms—such as your depression about your anxiety and your anxiety about your depression.
3. *Understand* that you have created your secondary symptoms— yes, *made* yourself panicked about your panic, self-hating about your self-hatred.
4. *Recognize* that because *you* brought on your secondary feelings of misery, *you* also have the ability to work at changing them. You strongly (emotionally) and persistently (actively) recognize this—use thinking, emotion, and action to do so.

What next?

Suppose that, using REBT, you have made yourself fully aware that you feel, let us say, anxiety about your anxiety—or panic about your panic! What do you do now?

Take these Disputing steps:

1. *Assume* that you created your panic about your panic with some absolutistic musts—such as, "I *must* not be panicked! I *have to* be calm!"
2. *Seek out, probe for* your *musts* until you find them: "Oh yes. I now see that I *do* believe that I *must* never be panicked, or else I'll end up in the loony bin. And that would *really* be *terrible!*"
3. Actively Dispute your musts until you come up with—and truly believe!—Effective Rational Philosophies. Like this:

iB (irrational beliefs)—"It's *awful* to be panicked!"

D (disputing)—"Where is the evidence that it's *awful?*"

E (effective rational philosophy)—"Nowhere except in my foolish thinking! It's *only* very inconvenient, but I can always stand it—and work to get rid of my panic about panic."

iB—"I *must* not be panicked!"

D—"Where is that law of the universe written?"

E—"Nowhere. Only in the heads of crooked-thinking humans like me! If the universe ruled that I must not be panicked, I couldn't possibly be. Obviously its rule is that I *can be* extremely anxious—if I allow myself to be!"

iB—"If I am panicked, I'll end up in the loony bin and that would *really* be terrible!"

D—"Is this true?"

E—"Nonsense! I and billions of other people have been panicked before and have somehow managed to stay out of the mental hospital. Feelings of panic are painful but rarely produce nervous breakdowns. Otherwise, all of us humans would be confined! And even if the worst comes to the worst—which is most unlikely—and I do for a while get hospitalized, that would be highly uncomfortable. But I can still survive, calm down, and lead a happy life. If I *think* I can!"

If you Dispute (D) your irrational Beliefs (iBs) leading to your emotional Consequences (C) of anxiety *about* anxiety, you can then keep *thinking and planning* to rid yourself of it and to see that you rarely bring it back. Your final conclusions will tend to be:

1. "I am never an *incompetent or rotten person* for making myself anxious and making myself anxious about my anxiety. I am merely a *person who* has some rotten philosophies—which I can work at changing."
2. "No matter how badly I inconvenience and handicap myself with feelings of stress and panic, they are *only* that: *inconvenient.* Never *awful* or *horrible!* Never *unbearable!* Only a royal pain in the neck!"

Once you keep making these conclusions, you can go back to your original feelings of panic (such as your horror about being rejected by someone); discover your irrational Beliefs that are creating the panic (for example, "I cannot be alone and be happy!"); and Dispute these iBs and remove your original anxiety.

Insight No. 6 of REBT, as you can see, indicates that you easily create primary emotional problems and secondary problems *about* your original ones. It encourages you to give up, first, your secondary neurosis—and then to undo your primary one.

Insight No. 6 also shows you how you can create third-level disturbances and how to work against them, too. Gerald, for example, first made himself anxious about doing well at work (primary problem). Then he became addicted to alcohol in order to temporarily calm his anxiety (secondary problem). Then he damned himself severely for his drinking (third-level problem). Because of his third-level self-blame he upset himself so much that he did worse at work and (to soothe his anxiety) drank much more.

If you heed Insight No. 6, you will undo your second-level and third-level emotional problems, then get back to working against your primary disturbances and thus comprehensively help yourself.

Here are some follow-ups on the clients mentioned previously in this chapter:

George examined his irrational Belief, "I *must* never be angry at my mother, even though she neglected me as a child and now demands that I devote myself to her in her old age. What a louse I am!" He first accepted *himself* with his anger—then, free of his self-hatred, he stopped demanding that his mother be nondemanding and gave up hatred of her (though not his dislike of her behavior).

Cynthia, after much rethinking, was able to strongly repeat to herself many times, "My continuing to smoke is indeed a bad weakness. But beating myself for smoking only makes me weaker! If *I* am no good for smoking, how can rotten *me* ever do a good thing like stopping? Never! So even if I keep foolishly smoking, I am determined to stop my self-beating!" As soon as she ceased her self-blaming, Cynthia found it much easier to stay at five cigarettes a day, instead of her usual two packs.

Josef acknowledged that his woman friend really was making it difficult—though not impossible—for him to assert himself. But by showing himself that she had a right, as a human being, to be wrong, he lost his anger at her—and then, despite his fear and discomfort, he was able to force himself to be more and more assertive, until acting that way became natural and easy.

Gerald, with the help of one of my regular therapy groups, first worked at his third-level problem—his downing himself for his alcoholism—by showing himself that his drinking was stupid but that *he* was not a stupid, hopeless person. Then he tackled his secondary symptom (low frustration tolerance), which accompanied his irrational Belief, "I can't stand feeling anxious, so I must immediately relieve myself by drinking!" Finally, he went back to his primary symptom, his anxiety created by his demand that he *had to* do very well at work—and he was able to make himself *concerned* but no longer *over*concerned about his job performances and to become much less anxious. On all three levels he improved—and his drinking and his work considerably improved, too. As his anxiety, low frustration tolerance, and self-damning decreased, he was able to stop drinking altogether and lead a much more productive life.

REBT Exercise No. 10

This is an exercise in self-honesty. Dishonesty with yourself is usually the result of your self-downing. You feel ashamed to admit the truth—as when you fail miserably at something or see that others are laughing at you—so you lie to yourself and deny your errors and your foolishness.

What you can do now is honestly admit when you recently felt upset—felt anxious, depressed, or enraged. For example:

- Were you anxious about your children or other close relatives coming home later than expected?
- Were you panicked about a pain in your chest, thinking it might be a heart attack?
- Were you depressed about the death of a relative or close friend?
- Were you enraged about terrorism directed against innocent civilians?

These are anxieties about real major or important events and you probably were able to accept your reactions and deal with them. But how about some recent minor or unimportant events? For example:

- You notice you have a spot on your shirt and are anxious about the strangers on the bus or subway who might notice it.
- You are at a party or a convention and forgot someone's name and are panicked lest that person see that you have forgotten it.
- You were unassertive with your barber and are afraid that people will discover that you let him cut your hair too short.
- You have to go to the bathroom in the midst of a concert and are ashamed that people will think you foolish and disruptive for going.

Look for minor incidents like these and acknowledge that you were really anxious, panicked, or ashamed about them—and that you were anxious about your anxiety, ashamed of your shame, depressed about your panic. Can you be quite honest with yourself? Can you fully admit your original panic about this slight failing or screw-up—and can you admit your secondary panic of letting people know about your original anxiety? Force yourself to be honest. If it kills you!

Now do something more.

1. Laugh to yourself about your panic and your panic about your panic. See how ridiculous it is that you absolutely *need* people's approval for almost everything you do—and that you need their approval for your needing their approval! See how funny this is!

2. As a shame-attacking exercise, tell someone—better, tell *several* people—about your "shameful" feelings. Let them know what a trivial thing you upset yourself about. Show them how you made yourself upset about your upsetness. Be ruthlessly open and honest to others about how afraid you are—and how fearful of your fearfulness!

3. Find your main *musts* about your original feelings of panic. For example: "I *must* remember this person's name! I *must* not have to ask him, once again, what his name is! I *must* not insult him by forgetting who he is! I *must* not let him know I stupidly forgot!"

4. Find your *musts* about your secondary anxiety. For example: "I *must* not show my anxiety to others! I *must* not be so anxious over trifles! I *must* get over my anxiety immediately!"
5. Rip up these musts and change them to preferences.
6. Continue to observe and admit that you often make yourself anxious or panicked over many little things. Continue to accept yourself with your anxiety, to often confess it to others, and to find and dispute the musts with which you create it.

To make things even clearer and prevent your confusion, let me emphasize again that your Belief System (B) always includes—as I said in 1956—thoughts, feelings, and action-tendencies. You seem to have *pure* Beliefs but they are mixed in with feelings and actions. You think-feel-behave and your thoughts *influence* your feelings and behaviors, your feelings *influence* your thoughts and behaviors, and your behaviors *influence* your thoughts and your feelings. All three are integrated and we falsely see them as separate. So when you think about your thinking—as you are uniquely able to do—you *also* think-feel-act about your thinking. You strongly or lightly (that is, *emotionally*) think about it; and you persistently, obsessively (that is, *actively*) think about it. Why? Because that is the way you are—a thinking-feeling-behaving creature. It is hard to keep this in mind, but you had better try to do so. If you *only* think and not *also* feel and behave about your irrational Beliefs, you will not truly "understand" them and change them. Thinking-feeling-behaving and the language we use to do them are confusing and often contradictory, and that is one reason why we do them destructively and why there may not be any perfect and permanent way to keep them in order. So you do your best to think-feel-and-act about your dysfunctional and irrational Beliefs—which, again, *include* thoughts, feelings, and actions—and you thereby make them *more* functional, but not *completely* functional and sane. You also *accept* your imperfections in doing this thinking-feeling-acting about your dysfunctional thinking-feeling-action and stubbornly refuse to upset yourself about upsetting yourself! Unconditional acceptance *includes* acceptance of your limitations! Too damned bad—but not awful!

12

REBT Insight No. 7: Solving Practical Problems as Well as Emotional Problems

Although REBT is often accused of being a superficial form of therapy—because its ABCs are simple and easy for almost anyone to understand—it actually is more comprehensive than most other therapies. For it sees everyone—including you—as affecting and being affected by the people and the environment around them.

You live in a social system—with your family, friends, business associates, acquaintances, and strangers. To some degree, you affect these others, and they affect and influence you.

You also live in an external environment—with air, vegetation, roads, buildings, weather conditions, machines, and autos. All of these, too, affect you; you, in turn, act on them.

Finally, you live in your own body—with bones, blood, internal organs, skin, nerves, and other tissues that strongly influence you. Again, your doings—such as eating, drinking, exercising, thinking, and feeling—importantly affect your body.

Living in this complicated environment, you have (as noted previously in this book) basic Goals (G), which you bring to the Activating Events of your life. These Goals create many practical problems for you to try to solve. Such as:

- How shall I get a good education?
- What shall I do to find a suitable mate?
- Which profession shall I choose and how shall I succeed at it?
- What recreations do I find enjoyable and worthy of my time and effort?

Once you recognize these reality problems, you can try to solve them—or you can foolishly choose to make yourself upset about them. If you upset yourself, you then have a problem about a problem—an emotional problem (or neurosis) about your reality problem (how to survive and enjoy yourself).

REBT is more systematic than most other therapies in that it encourages you to tackle both your original practical difficulties and your later emotional difficulties—though not necessarily in that order. In fact, it often encourages you, when you have a neurotic problem, to first work at solving that dilemma—and then to tackle your practical problems.

Why so? For several reasons:

1. While you are anxious or depressed about making a decision—such as, "Shall I stay with my love partner or end our relationship?"—you may be unable to see which of your desires (to stay or leave) is greater. Your guilt about leaving, for example, may prevent you from seeing that you really want to go. Or your anger at your partner may push aside your real desire to stay.
2. You may spend so much time and energy being disturbed that you have little left to devote to solving your practical problem. Thus, you may spend so much time whining about having to decide whether to leave your love partner that you never get around to actually making a clear decision.
3. You may be so upset about having a practical problem and knowing no good and quick solution to it that you may not be able to keep your thoughts in order to help solve it.

REBT, therefore, encourages you first to solve your emotional upsetness (your problem about a problem) and then carefully consider your practical decisions.

This brings us to REBT's Insight No. 7: *As you attempt to solve your practical life problems, look carefully to discover whether you have any emotional problems—such as feelings of anxiety or depression—about these practical issues. If so, seek out and actively Dispute your dogmatic, musturbatory thinking-feeling-behaving that leads to your emotional difficulties. While working to reduce your neurotic feelings, go back to your practical difficulties and use effective self-management and problem-solving methods to tackle them.*

Joani greatly wanted to finish college but had little money and had to commute fifty miles to do so. Rough going! But she made it much rougher by telling herself, "I *must* finish college and do so soon! This means that I have to work hard at my job and at school, and also spend time commuting—and that's unfair and things *shouldn't* be that unfair! Besides, my father keeps telling me that I haven't the ability to finish—and maybe he's right. If so, that would be *awful* and I'd *never* get any of the good things I really want in life! I hate my rotten father for doing this to me!"

With these strong irrational Beliefs, Joani took her original practical problems and used them to make herself feel anxious, depressed, angry, and self-hating. Naturally, her disturbed feelings greatly interfered with her solving her practical (money, school, work, and commuting) problems—not to mention her trouble communicating with her father.

Joani and I first worked at revealing and changing her dogmatic musts about herself, about her father, and about the school situation. Then, as we did this, I helped her improve her practical problem skills and figure out alternate solutions that her upsetness blocked her from discovering—including borrowing money and living and working closer to her college. I also helped her to learn communication skills (to get along better with her father) and to acquire organizing and study skills (and thus be capable of doing more schoolwork in less time).

You, too, can first change your irrational Beliefs and the disturbed emotional Consequences to which they lead. You can then go back to A (the Activating Events or Adversities of your life) and use the problem-solving and other skills to make your decisions more practical and pleasurable.

To improve your life, you can use REBT to acquire assertiveness training, time-management methods, relationship skills, sex education, job advancement methods, and various other skills that may help you lead a more self-fulfilling existence. Because REBT deals with thinking *and* behavior and because it includes corrective teaching, it is a pioneering problem-solving and skill-training approach to therapy.

Which once again shows that it is comprehensive! It is a "systems theory" of human behavior that is truly systematic! By helping you to understand your disruptive feelings (C) about your life events (A), and to change your ideas (B) that produce these feelings, it enables you to work at recognizing your As, Bs, and Cs. And to see and rearrange the complicated ways in which A, B, and C interact.

REBT Exercise No. 11

Think of a practical problem that you want to solve or a decision you want to make. For example, consider:

How to get a better job

How to give a good speech

How to win a golf game

How to write a term paper

How to drive to a strange city

How to relate well to others

How to have more enjoyable sex

Think about these decisions:

Which TV set to buy

Which house to purchase

Which person to choose as a partner in a game

Which courses to take at school

Which suit or dress to wear to a party

Which life career to choose

Which exercise program to select

Look for any emotional-behavioral problems that you have about these practical problems. Examples include:

- Are you anxious about getting a good job and keeping it?
- Would you be ashamed if you gave a poor speech?
- Would you be depressed if you played golf poorly?
- Are you continuing to procrastinate about writing a term paper?
- Are you angry about driving in a strange city?
- Are you afraid to try to relate to others?
- Do you blame yourself severely for having sex problems?
- Do you compulsively keep getting more and more information about TV sets before you decide to buy one?
- Are you extremely fearful that the house you purchase will collapse or be burned down?
- Do you mercilessly blame yourself for picking the wrong partner in a game?
- Do you keep changing your school courses even after the term has begun?
- Do you agonize over choosing a suit or dress to wear to a party?
- Do you do nothing about choosing a career?
- Do you try one exercise program after another and quit before it really gets underway?

If you are anxious, ashamed, depressed, or enraged about your practical problems or if you are indecisive, phobic, or compulsive about making decisions, look for your dogmatic demands—for your shoulds, oughts, and musts, and for your awfulizing, self-downing, and I-can't-stand-it-itis that accompany them.

Examples

"I *must* get a good job and *have to* keep it when I do!"

"My speech *must* come off marvelously! It would be shameful if they laugh at me when I give it!"

"I *should* have played that golf game better! What a hopelessly rotten athlete I am!"

"Writing that damned term paper *ought to be* easier! I *can't stand* the hassle of doing it! I'll do it later!"

"These blasted city streets *should be* laid out better, with much clearer signs! How *awful* that they are giving me needless trouble!"

"I *must* get the very best TV set for the money! I *can't bear it* if I get gypped!"

"Suppose something dreadful happens to a house after I purchase it! I *must have a guarantee* that everything will be all right with it!"

"I'll never forgive myself if I pick the wrong partner for this game. What a complete idiot I would be!"

"I *must* have the best course and the best teacher. It would be *horrible* if I wasted my time in this course. If I don't change it right away, even though it's against the school rules, I'm a perfect wimp!"

"If I choose the wrong suit or dress for this party and people laugh at me for picking it, I might as well kill myself!"

"Every possible career I choose has too many hassles that go with it. I *can't* bear any career with so many hassles!"

"I *shouldn't* have to keep exercising but should be perfectly healthy without doing it!"

Actively dispute your shoulds and musts, your awfulizing, your can't-stand-it-itis, and your self-downing. Consider the folllowing:

Disputing: "Why *must* I get a good job and where is it written that I *have to* keep it when I do?"

Answer: "I don't *have to* get or keep a good job, but very much *want* to. So I'll keep pushing to get one."

Disputing: "Where is it written that my speech *must* come off marvelously? How would it be shameful if they laugh at me when I give it?"

Answer: "It is not written anywhere—except in the foolish scripts I write for myself! It would be unfortunate if they laughed at me when I gave it, but only my speech would be bad and I would not be a *bad, incompetent, shameful person.*

Disputing: "Why *should* I have played that golf game better? How does playing it badly make me a hopelessly rotten athlete?"

Answer: "No reason why I *should* or *must* play it better, but it would be great if I did! It only shows that I was rotten at playing golf this time and not that I *never* would be good at playing it or any other sport!"

Disputing: "Prove that doing the term paper *ought to be* easier. In what way can't I *stand* the hassle of doing it?"

Answer: "Doing the paper *ought to be* just as bad as it is. For that's the way it is right now. I don't like the hassle of doing it, but I'll like even less the hassles that stem from *not* doing it. So back to the drawing board!"

Disputing: "Can I show why the blasted city streets *should be* laid out better, with much clearer signs? Is it really *awful* that it's giving me this much trouble?"

Answer: "I can only show that it would be lovely if the city streets were laid out better and had much clearer signs. But I cannot show that this is *necessary*, because if it were these streets *would* be laid out to suit me. Obviously, the city planners do not care the way I want them to care. Tough! But I can still find my way around!"

Disputing: "*Must* I really get the best TV set for the money? *Can't* I bear it if I get gypped?"

Answer: "No, I clearly don't *have to* get the best set for the money. I *can* end up with an inferior one. And if I actually get gypped and end up with an inferior set, I can *still* get a lot of pleasure out of it. That would be too bad—but it would still be more good than bad.

And if I don't take the risk and buy one of the sets available, I'll never enjoy TV at all! So I'd better choose one!"

Disputing: "Do I really *need* a guarantee that everything will be all right with any house that I purchase? Will the world come to an end if something dreadful happens to it?"

Answer: "No, it would be great if I had such a guarantee—but guarantees like that simply don't exist. All I can get is a high degree of probability that any house I purchase will last a long time in spite of all the things that could happen to it. And even if the house somehow gets demolished, my life will go on and I can still enjoy it."

Disputing: "Can I forgive myself if I pick the wrong partner for this game and consequently we lose the match? Would picking the wrong partner make me an idiot?"

Answer: "Of course I can forgive myself for making a poor choice of a partner. That would be a foolish act, but it would hardly make me a totally stupid person. Since I am fallible, I will often make foolish choices, but I will not *always* make them or be *damnable* for making them. I can decide to accept myself, if not my poor decisions, and thereby prepare myself to learn and make better decisions in the future."

Disputing: "Do I *really* have to take the best course and have the best teacher? Does it *truly* make me a wimp if I don't rebel against the school rules and make them change my courses?"

Answer: "No, it is obviously unnecessary for me to take the best course and to have the best teacher, though that would be highly desirable. If I go along with the school rules and don't make them change my course, I won't be acting wimpishly but merely will be following normal restrictions. And even if I do act weakly, that never makes me a *total wimp* or a *weak person.*"

Disputing: "Why does every possible career I choose have too many hassles that go with it? Where is the evidence that I can't bear any career with so many hassles?"

Answer: "Just about any career I choose will have *many* hassles but not *too* many. Because it is the nature of careers to have hassles—

they all do! Too bad—but unless I accept such hassles I'll end up with *no* career—and thus have *worse* problems! I may never *like* the difficulties of a career I choose, but I definitely can *stand* them. And I'd damned well better do so—if I want any career at all!"

Once you find your irrational Beliefs (iBs) that interfere with your solving your practical problem and from making good decisions, then go back to these original problems and do your best to solve them.

Write down a good many problem-solving questions, such as these, on any practical problems you wish to solve:

- What should I do to get a good job?
- What step had I better take first?
- What steps shall I take next?
- Who should I consult about getting a good job?
- Can any of my friends possibly help me?
- What kind of a résumé—or several résumés—shall I write?
- How can I get help with my résumés?
- Shall I let my past employers know I am looking, to be fully sure they give me good references?
- What shall I do to have better job interviews?

Now, outline—and preferably put on paper—your answers. Then make a plan to act on and to implement these ideas. Then follow this plan—yes, *push yourself* to follow this plan.

If everything goes well, fine. Continue to solve your practical problems and issues. If you don't follow your plan, or follow it poorly, or make yourself upset about the results of following it, assume that you have some emotional difficulties about your practical difficulties—and go back to the ABCs of REBT, again, to see what they are and how you can deal with them. As you keep resolving your emotional problems, go back, once again, to your practical questions to work out, as above, solutions for them. Keep shuttling back and forth from your practical to your emotional and once again your practical problems. And don't expect any perfect or super-marvelous solutions. For that silly expectation will only enhance your emotional dilemmas and make everything much worse!

REBT Exercise No. 12

You cannot very well solve practical problems or make good decisions without taking some risks. Typical risks include:

- Taking too long to solve a problem or make a decision
- Spending too much time and energy to solve it or to decide on a solution
- Taking too little time and trouble to plan and decide what to do
- Picking the wrong decision and having to live with it
- Doing well with your practical problems at first and later failing at them
- Finding a fairly good solution but not a great one, which you would really like to find.

If you tend to be overconcerned about solving a problem or making a decision and to take too much time and energy with it, free yourself to take the risk of planning and deciding on it more quickly. Thus, give yourself a limited amount of time to make up your job résumé, to get a list of people to send it to, to send out letters to these people, and to start going on job interviews. Don't prepare too much. Take the chance that you may do poorly. Show yourself that you can learn by your errors and probably do better next time.

If, when you force yourself to plan and decide on some important tasks quickly, you refuse to do so or you achieve this goal and upset yourself because your plans and decisions are not good *enough*, fill out an REBT Self-Help Form about your emotional problem. (See Figures 1 and 2.)

Figure 1. Blank REBT Self-Help Form

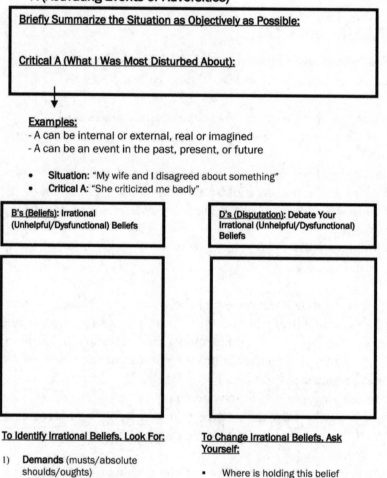

A (Activating Events or Adversities)

Briefly Summarize the Situation as Objectively as Possible:

Critical A (What I Was Most Disturbed About):

Examples:
- A can be internal or external, real or imagined
- A can be an event in the past, present, or future

- **Situation:** "My wife and I disagreed about something"
- **Critical A:** "She criticized me badly"

B's (Beliefs): Irrational (Unhelpful/Dysfunctional) Beliefs

D's (Disputation): Debate Your Irrational (Unhelpful/Dysfunctional) Beliefs

To Identify Irrational Beliefs, Look For:

1) **Demands** (musts/absolute shoulds/oughts)
2) **Awfulizing/Catastrophizing** (It's awful, terrible, horrible!)
3) **Frustration Intolerance** (I can't stand it!)
4) **Self-Downing, Other-Downing, or Life-Downing** (I'm bad or worthless, He/she is bad or worthless, or Life is not worthwhile)

© Windy Dryden & Jane Walker, 1992. Revised by Albert Ellis, 1996. Revised by Windy Dryden & Daniel David, 2009.

To Change Irrational Beliefs, Ask Yourself:

- Where is holding this belief getting me? **Is it helpful** or getting me into trouble?
- **Where is the evidence** to support my irrational belief?
  - o   Is it really awful (as bad as it could be)?
  - o   Can I really not stand it?
  - o   Am I really a totally bad person?
- **Is it logical?** Does it follow from my preferences?
- **Use metaphorical disputation**

C (Consequences)

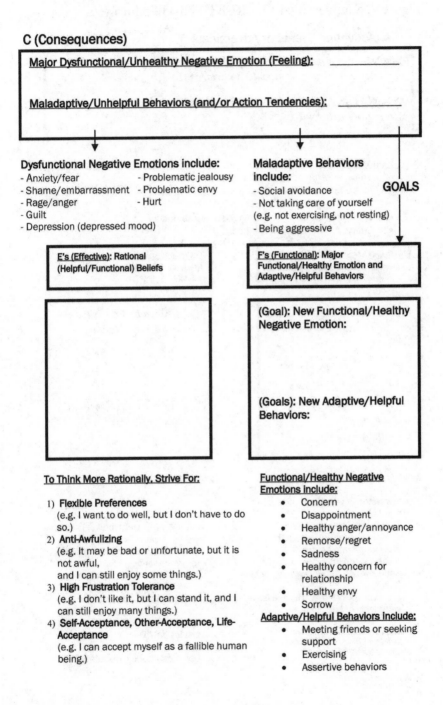

Major Dysfunctional/Unhealthy Negative Emotion (Feeling): _____

Maladaptive/Unhelpful Behaviors (and/or Action Tendencies): _____

Dysfunctional Negative Emotions include:
- Anxiety/fear
- Shame/embarrassment
- Rage/anger
- Guilt
- Depression (depressed mood)
- Problematic jealousy
- Problematic envy
- Hurt

Maladaptive Behaviors include:
- Social avoidance
- Not taking care of yourself
  (e.g. not exercising, not resting)
- Being aggressive

GOALS

E's (Effective): Rational (Helpful/Functional) Beliefs

F's (Functional): Major Functional/Healthy Emotion and Adaptive/Helpful Behaviors

(Goal): New Functional/Healthy Negative Emotion:

(Goals): New Adaptive/Helpful Behaviors:

To Think More Rationally, Strive For:

1) **Flexible Preferences**
   (e.g. I want to do well, but I don't have to do so.)
2) **Anti-Awfulizing**
   (e.g. It may be bad or unfortunate, but it is not awful,
   and I can still enjoy some things.)
3) **High Frustration Tolerance**
   (e.g. I don't like it, but I can stand it, and I can still enjoy many things.)
4) **Self-Acceptance, Other-Acceptance, Life-Acceptance**
   (e.g. I can accept myself as a fallible human being.)

Functional/Healthy Negative Emotions include:
- Concern
- Disappointment
- Healthy anger/annoyance
- Remorse/regret
- Sadness
- Healthy concern for relationship
- Healthy envy
- Sorrow

Adaptive/Helpful Behaviors include:
- Meeting friends or seeking support
- Exercising
- Assertive behaviors

Figure 2. Sample Filled-Out REBT Self-Help Form

A (Activating Events or Adversities)

Briefly Summarize the Situation as Objectively as Possible:
My boss asked to see me at the end of the day

Critical A (What I Was Most Disturbed About):
He is going to criticize me

Examples:
- A can be internal or external, real or imagined
- A can be an event in the past, present, or future

- **Situation:** "My wife and I disagreed about something"
- **Critical A:** "She criticized me badly"

B's (Beliefs): Irrational (Unhelpful/Dysfunctional) Beliefs	D's (Disputation): Debate Your Irrational (Unhelpful/Dysfunctional) Beliefs
My boss must not criticize me (Demand) *It will be awful if he criticizes me (Awfulizing)*	*Do I have to be immune from such criticism?* *Is it bad or is it awful if he criticizes me?*

To Identify Irrational Beliefs, Look For:

1) **Demands** (musts/absolute shoulds/oughts)
2) **Awfulizing/Catastrophizing** (It's awful, terrible, horrible!)
3) **Frustration Intolerance** (I can't stand it!)
4) **Self-Downing, Other-Downing, or Life-Downing** (I'm bad or worthless, He/she is bad or worthless, or Life is not worthwhile)

© Windy Dryden & Jane Walker, 1992. Revised by Albert Ellis, 1996. Revised by Windy Dryden & Daniel David, 2009.

To Change Irrational Beliefs, Ask Yourself:

- Where is holding this belief getting me? **Is it helpful** or getting me into trouble?
- **Where is the evidence** to support my irrational belief?
  - Is it really awful (as bad as it could be)?
  - Can I really not stand it?
  - Am I really a totally bad person?
- **Is it logical?** Does it follow from my preferences?
- **Use metaphorical disputation**

C (Consequences)

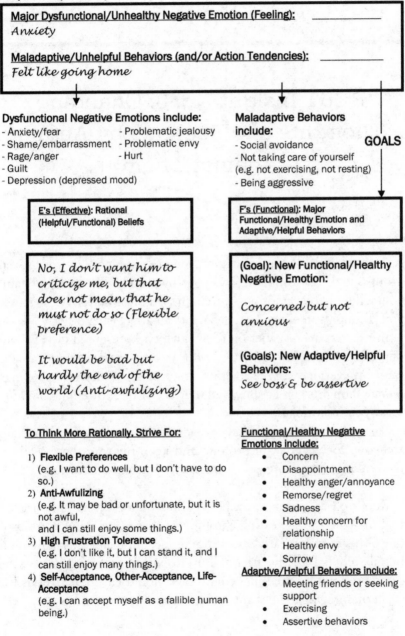

Major Dysfunctional/Unhealthy Negative Emotion (Feeling): _____
Anxiety

Maladaptive/Unhelpful Behaviors (and/or Action Tendencies): _____
Felt like going home

Dysfunctional Negative Emotions include:
- Anxiety/fear
- Shame/embarrassment
- Rage/anger
- Guilt
- Depression (depressed mood)
- Problematic jealousy
- Problematic envy
- Hurt

Maladaptive Behaviors include:
- Social avoidance
- Not taking care of yourself
(e.g. not exercising, not resting)
- Being aggressive

GOALS

E's (Effective): Rational (Helpful/Functional) Beliefs

No, I don't want him to criticize me, but that does not mean that he must not do so (Flexible preference)

It would be bad but hardly the end of the world (Anti-awfulizing)

F's (Functional): Major Functional/Healthy Emotion and Adaptive/Helpful Behaviors

(Goal): New Functional/Healthy Negative Emotion:

Concerned but not anxious

(Goals): New Adaptive/Helpful Behaviors:
See boss & be assertive

To Think More Rationally, Strive For:

1) **Flexible Preferences**
(e.g. I want to do well, but I don't have to do so.)
2) **Anti-Awfulizing**
(e.g. It may be bad or unfortunate, but it is not awful, and I can still enjoy some things.)
3) **High Frustration Tolerance**
(e.g. I don't like it, but I can stand it, and I can still enjoy many things.)
4) **Self-Acceptance, Other-Acceptance, Life-Acceptance**
(e.g. I can accept myself as a fallible human being.)

Functional/Healthy Negative Emotions include:
- Concern
- Disappointment
- Healthy anger/annoyance
- Remorse/regret
- Sadness
- Healthy concern for relationship
- Healthy envy
- Sorrow

Adaptive/Helpful Behaviors include:
- Meeting friends or seeking support
- Exercising
- Assertive behaviors

13

REBT Insight No. 8: Changing
Thoughts and Feelings by Acting
Against Them

As I noted in the previous chapter, you are influenced by your social
groups, your environment, and your own body. But to understand
yourself and your emotional problems, you had better also see that
your thoughts, feelings, and behaviors all affect each other.

In my first major paper on REBT, which I presented in 1956 and
published in the *Journal of General Psychology*, I stated that humans
rarely, if ever, have *pure* thoughts, emotions, or behaviors. Feelings
include thoughts and actions, and they are also followed by thoughts
about your emotions.

Particularly when you have steady feelings—as when you hate
someone for years—you prolong and keep reviving these feelings
by thinking, imagining, and rating what you and others do.

Roberto was beaten by his father when he was fifteen and insisted
that the pain of the beating and the fact that it was done in front of
one of his friends clearly *caused* him to feel enraged at his father and
humiliated before his friend. But Roberto was wrong—because
some boys, under the same conditions, would have felt anxious instead of enraged and defiant rather than ashamed. So Roberto very

likely *created* his rage and shame by thinking, within a few seconds of being beaten by his father:

1. "That bastard *shouldn't* beat me like this, especially when I haven't done anything wrong!"
2. "My friend must think I am a weakling for letting my father beat me. I *shouldn't* be so weak! How shameful it is for me to let my father get away with this unfair beating!"

Roberto didn't remember, when I saw him fourteen years later, thinking anything like this—and sometimes insisted that he *automatically*, without any thinking on his part, became angry and ashamed because of his father's unfair beating in front of his friend. I showed him that we rarely feel without thinking, and he partially accepted this.

He was much more convinced when I showed him that he had kept alive his feelings with hate-creating thoughts like: "How *could* my father have been so cruel and unjust to me when I was in no position to fight him back? He *shouldn't* have done an awful thing like that! That bastard!" And every time he contacted his father, he *continued* to upset himself with thoughts like, "Even though I was much smaller and weaker than he at that time, I *should* have done my best to bite him, kick him in the balls, or do something to stop him! How shameful that I didn't!"

Moral: pure feelings rarely, if ever, exist. And even if they do—if you see an object flying at you and you immediately, without a thought, feel panicked—your feelings last for a few seconds and do not develop into real disturbances. Unless you *then* have irrational Beliefs *about* them. Such as: "Hell! That object almost killed me—as it *must* not do!" Or: "I *shouldn't* be panicked! How foolish of me to panic like this!"

So, whenever you feel emotionally upset, look for your musturbatory thinking that is at the bottom of your upsetness—track down your silly demands and strive to change them.

But, says REBT, just as your thoughts create feelings and behaviors, the latter also affect your thinking. When Roberto raged at his

father, he could hardly think straight and he "unthinkingly" did
foolish things—such as stubbornly refusing to lend his father rent
money and thereby harming his mother, whom he loved.

So thoughts, feelings, and behaviors interact with and circularly
affect each other. Crazy ideas create frantic feelings and strange acts.
Hysterical feelings bring on foolish notions and behaviors. Rash actions produce nutty convictions and insane deeds. Thoughts, moreover, lead to other thoughts, feelings to new feelings, actions to
different actions. The influence of thoughts, emotions, and activities on each other never seems to stop!

Suppose you want to change your obsessions, compulsions, phobias, and addictions. What then? Well, no one method will work for
you all of the time. Sometimes using one philosophy to rid yourself
of your anxiety will work—and sometimes it won't. Often, fully expressing your feelings will considerably help you—and often deliberately avoiding your feelings, and instead distracting yourself with
some intellectual pursuit, will serve you better. At times, you will
best ward off disturbances by trying every therapeutic method you
can think of—the long and the short and the tall!

Give up any prejudices about which technique *should* or *must*
work. Freely experiment! Try almost any treatment plan that seems
sound for a reasonable length of time. But don't necessarily stick
with it forever. You are not *any* seeker after help, or an *average* trou-
bled person. You are *you*—and what goes for, or against, you is not
the same as what is good or bad for anyone else. Remember *that* as
you go about your self-therapy experiments.

There practically never is one and only one helpful way.
According to REBT, you can often find one *main*, most *elegant* path
to undo your neurotic difficulties. (that is, make a profound change
in your thinking that will curtail your upsetness, keep it from coming back, and prevent you from manufacturing new emotional
problems in the future).

Fine: let us for the moment grant this. Even then, there is no *one*
way for you to produce this new dramatic outlook. Many roads lead
to Rome!

As I pointed out in 1962 in *Reason and Emotion in Psychotherapy*, and as Joseph Wolpe, Hans Eysenck, Isaac Marks, Albert Bandura, Stanley Rachman, and other behavior therapists later asserted, sometimes the best—or indeed the only—way to change a fixed idea is to force yourself to *act* against it: to engage in *live* homework assignments. This kind of forced—yes, *forced*—activity may show you that you *can* surrender an obsessive, compulsive, or frightful belief. Similarly, if you work directly on your feelings, and vividly experience and express them, you may more thoroughly change your crooked thoughts than by directly disputing these irrational Beliefs.

Let us, then, state Insight No. 8: *You can change irrational Beliefs (iBs) and disruptive feelings by acting against them: by performing behaviors that contradict them.*

In fact, it is doubtful if you ever truly change an irrational Belief until you literally act (and act *many times*) against it. Similarly, you practically never permanently stop your compulsive behaviors until you *think* about changing them and *decide* to do so—again and again!

Some psychologists have spread the tale that REBT was at first purely intellectual and that it only later added behavioral methods. Fiction! I was a cognitive-behavior sex therapist in 1943 when I first started to do psychotherapy, and I wrote pioneering papers on active-directive sex therapy in the 1940s and 1950s. In addition, I summarized some of this material in my 1954 book, *The American Sexual Tragedy*—which was denounced by many passive Freudian and Rogerian therapists. Although I largely abandoned behavioral methods when I practiced psychoanalysis between 1949 and 1953, I found psychoanalysis incredibly inefficient and therefore went back to cognitive-behavioral methods in 1953 as I was beginning to create REBT.

My strong bias in favor of behavior therapy stemmed from my successful experiments with myself when I was nineteen years old and had no idea of becoming a therapist. I often tell the story of how, being unusually shy of speaking in public, I forced myself, for three months, to give many political talks.

I told myself, following several philosophers, that nothing terrible would happen to me if I spoke badly. I followed the teachings of the pioneer behavior therapist, John B. Watson, who showed that *active* reconditioning, or forcing yourself to keep doing what you are afraid of doing, really rids you of irrational fears. So I expected—intellectually!—to overcome my fear of public speaking. And I did.

However—surprise, surprise!—I unexpectedly began to *enjoy* speaking in public and have had fun doing it for the next sixty-five years. To my astonishment, I made a 180-degree turnabout of my extreme fear.

Seeing that forcing myself to do uncomfortable things worked, I decided to do the same with my enormous fear of meeting new women. Because of my terrible fear of rejection, I never—and I mean *never*—approached strange women, although I went to walk and read in the Bronx Botanical Gardens about 250 days a year and saw a number of desirable women with whom I was eager to talk and date, and who also seemed to be flirting with me.

So I gave myself the activity homework assignment of talking to every young woman I found sitting alone on one of the park benches. No exceptions! No cop-outs!

Although very fearful and uncomfortable, I forced myself to carry out this assignment—made myself open a conversation with over one hundred women in a single month. Yes, one hundred "stranger" encounters—the kind I had always wanted to make but had fearfully avoided up to that time.

I received no direct reward from these pick-ups—since only one of these one hundred females made a date with me and she never showed up!—but I completely overcame my fear of encountering strange women and have been able to talk to them easily ever since. For by getting rejected so many times, I *saw* that nothing dreadful happened—no name calling, no vomiting and running away and screaming, no calling a cop! And I *concluded* that I *could* talk to strange women, fail to date them, and *still* lead a highly enjoyable existence.

I also saw that behavioral methods—particularly *acting* against one's fears—often work better to change irrational Beliefs than do purely intellectual methods. And when I later found that psychoanalysis helped my clients very little and that talking them out of their irrational Beliefs (iBs) helped much more, I also realized that there are *many* ways of changing human attitudes—and that actively doing-what-you-are-scared-witless-of-doing is one of the best.

So, from its start, REBT has always included a variety of thinking, affective, and action methods. Over the years, it has added many therapy techniques, but it was decidedly multimodal (to use Arnold Lazarus's term) from the start.

Ironically, although the outstanding behavior therapist, Joseph Wolpe, consistently opposed "cognitive" therapy, his famous systematic desensitization technique uses imagination, teaching, and other forms of thinking. REBT, however, prefers more risk-taking activity homework assignments and is therefore *more* behavioral than many popular behavior therapies.

In the case of Roberto, noted at the beginning of this chapter, he agreed to often do the homework of Disputing his irrational Beliefs that his father absolutely *should not* have beaten him when he was a child and that he positively *ought not* have been a "weakling" who let his father get away with these beatings. I also helped him devise and carry out two activity homework assignments: (a) keep talking to his father regularly instead of (as he had been doing) completely avoiding him and (b) stand up to him in a firm but unhostile manner instead of backing down or screaming at him (as he had usually done before).

As a result of this combined thinking and behavioral REBT approach, Roberto gave up his rage toward his father and himself within a period of seven weeks. He continues to work on being tolerant and self-accepting several years after his therapy sessions ended.

REBT Exercise No. 13

Think of something you are irrationally afraid of doing, such as:

Speaking poorly in public

Writing an inadequate essay or report

Drawing badly

Being rejected by someone you care for

Riding in a fast elevator

Breaking into an ongoing conversation

Dancing in public

Talking to strangers

Taking a difficult course

Being laughed at by others

Playing a game or sport badly

Force yourself to do one of the things that you most fear and try to do it many times in rapid succession. Once you decide to do it, don't hesitate, or cop out. Do it and do it and do it!

While you are doing this "fearful" thing, show yourself that it is not really dangerous or fearful. Show yourself that:

- You will hardly die of doing it.
- You will be in no real physical danger.
- You may come to enjoy it.
- You can learn by doing it.
- You will add to your life by conquering your irrational fear.
- You will have the great challenge of overcoming it.
- You will eliminate the endless restrictions and frustrations of indulging in your fear.
- You will be working at disciplining yourself and overcoming your low frustration tolerance.
- You will behave more efficiently as you overcome this fear.
- You will gain more approval from others.
- You will help ward off physical and psychosomatic ailments, such as ulcers and high blood pressure.
- You will greatly reduce your negative feelings of anxiety, depression, self-downing, and self-pity.
- You will find life on the whole much more enjoyable.

REBT Exercise No. 13A

You may not see that you irrationally fear or are anxious about certain acts, but see yourself, instead, as being ashamed, embarrassed, or humiliated to perform them. Thus, you may not see yourself as being "afraid" to wear an unstylish dress or jacket or of telling someone about one of your weaknesses, but you may never do these things because you feel they are "shameful," "embarrassing," or "humiliating."

REBT considers feelings of shame or humiliation illegitimate because they almost always include a rational element ("I did something people consider wrong or stupid, and I would not like people to disapprove of me for doing it") and they also include an irrational or self-downing statement ("Therefore, I am a rotten or stupid person").

To combat this second, irrational element of shame, I created, in the late 1960s, my famous shame-attacking exercise—which is designed to help people stop feeling irrationally ashamed of anything, even when they perform and are disapproved of for some silly, stupid, inconvenient, weak, or foolish act.

To help you act against your irrational Beliefs and disturbed feelings, you can benefit from doing some shame-attacking exercises. To do so, you select something that you personally feel is shameful or embarrassing to do in public. Examples include:

- Dress inappropriately.
- Say something foolish to a group of people.
- Confess some weakness that people usually despise, such as, "I can't spell well."
- Act strangely, such as singing in the street or holding up a black umbrella on a sunny day.
- Yell out the stops on a train or bus.
- Tell someone that something is radically wrong with you, such as, "I just got out of the mental hospital. What month is this?"
- Say something that is unusually sexy, such as saying to a male or female companion in a loud voice so that others can hear, "Wasn't it great that we had sex five times last night?"

- Refuse to tip a waiter or cabdriver who has given you poor service.
- Return food to the kitchen of a restaurant when it is badly done.
- Walk a banana on a leash, as if it were a pet dog.
- Try to get a watch fixed in a shoe-repair shop.
- Ask people for a left-handed monkey wrench.

When you do this act that you consider silly or shameful, make sure that, first, you do not get into any real trouble. For example, don't expose yourself publicly and risk getting arrested; don't tell your boss that he or she is a worm and therefore risk getting fired.

Second, don't do anything that would harm someone else, such as slapping someone in the face or continue to bother someone.

The main thing to keep in mind as you do this shame-attacking exercise is to work on yourself while doing it so that you do *not* feel ashamed or humiliated even when others clearly disapprove of you. You can stubbornly *refuse* to feel ashamed by using self-statements.

Examples:

"So people think I am stupid or foolish. Too bad! Let them think so!"

"Actually, by doing this 'shameful' act I am helping myself overcome my self-downing. And that is great!"

"What I am doing may well be foolish but that doesn't make *me* a fool!"

"I am sorry that people think I am wrong for doing this thing, but that is only a disadvantage and is hardly the end of the world!"

"I know exactly why I am doing this act that I consider shameful, and therefore I can view it differently and see that it may be peculiar, but that doesn't mean that I am a peculiar or *incompetent person.* I am just a *person who* is choosing to act strangely in this instance."

Do this shame-attacking exercise and preferably do it many times until you feel thoroughly unashamed of doing it and even feel comfortable with it. Observe how your feelings and attitudes about "shameful" acts distinctly change as you keep doing these exercises.

14

REBT Insight No. 9: Using Work and Practice

In my book, *Reason and Emotion in Psychotherapy*, I pointed out that REBT includes three main insights, which are quite different from psychoanalytic insights. The first two REBT insights are:

1. You largely upset yourself at point C (Consequences) and do not only *get* upset by others or by events at point A (Activating Events or Adversities), and you do so by accepting or inventing irrational Beliefs (iBs).
2. No matter when, how, and why you originally made yourself anxious or depressed, you remain so today because you *still* consciously or unconsciously hold iBs.

We have been talking about and expanding these REBT insights so far and have added the insight that although as a child you were limited in your ability to see and change your irrational Beliefs, you now have considerable ability to do so—if you *see* and *use* the eight expanded insights discussed in the previous pages.

We now proceed to REBT's original Insight No. 3, which in our expanded version we shall call Insight No. 9: *No matter how clearly you see that you upset yourself and make yourself needlessly miserable, you rarely will improve except through work and practice—yes, considerable work and practice—to actively change your disturbance-creating Beliefs and feelings and to vigorously (and often uncomfortably) act against them.*

Insight No. 9 presents the Achilles' heel (and the Catch-22) of all therapies, including REBT. For it is easy for you to adopt and create self-defeating philosophies and to embed them into your actions and inactions. Damned easy! Because you tend to unconsciously and effortlessly make yourself miserable. In fact, in addition to your self-actualizing tendencies, you have a fine talent for self-defeat. Alas!

Insight No. 9 of REBT tells you that, yes—definitely, yes—you *can* work to change your miserable thoughts, feelings, and behaviors. But it doesn't necessarily make it *easy* to do so!

However, Insight No. 9 at least gives you a good chance to change. For it clearly states that if you are willing to work and practice—and to *continue* to work and practice—to surrender your irrational Beliefs and actions, you will most likely (I would say you are about 98 percent likely) to make yourself much less miserable.

Insight No. 9 shows how REBT differs from most other awareness-oriented psychotherapies, for several cognitive therapies were devised before REBT—those of Pierre Janet, Emile Coué, Paul Dubois, and Alfred Adler.

But these intellectual therapies fail to stress behavioral methods of changing personality. They often forget that to change your ideas, you had better persistently work at doing so—since you are born and reared to think crookedly and to unconsciously slip into rigid *shoulds* and *musts*. Even when you clearly *see* your *must*urbation and therefore give it up, you easily fall back, again and again, to dogmatic thinking.

Moreover, unless you repeatedly *act* against a phobic belief, you rarely eliminate it. If you are anxious about making friendly overtures to someone and you avoid making them, every time you "escape" from this "fearful" situation, you unconsciously reinforce your phobia. By running away, you actually tell yourself, whether or not you realize what you are thinking, "It *would* be awful if I were rejected! I must be *sure* I will be accepted before I try again." So you become more afraid.

On the other hand, if you keep making friendly overtures in spite of your horror or rejection, you usually see that nothing "horrible" happens, and you greatly help yourself overcome your phobia.

If we wish to put most neurotic problems under two main headings, we can call them (a) ego disturbance (self-damning) and (b) frustration intolerance (FI) or discomfort disturbance. Ego disturbance arises when you strongly believe, "*I* must do well and win others' approval, and *I* am an inadequate, undeserving person when I don't do as well as I *must*." This is really grandiosity—since you are demanding that you be *special, outstanding, perfect, superhuman*—which, of course, you will rarely be!

Discomfort disturbance is also godlike because the main philosophy behind it is: "Since I am such a special person who *needs* to have my main wants and interests gratified, other people *must* give me exactly what I desire and conditions *must* be nicely arranged to cater to my wishes. If not, it's *awful*, I *can't stand it*, and life is hardly worth living!"

So one major idea leading to discomfort disturbance is: "My life *must* be easy and people *have to* give me everything I truly crave." This can then lead to a related irrational Belief: "In order to make my life completely satisfying, I *must* always do well and *have to* win the love of all significant people all the time!" These ideas create FI. But they also involve ego because they insist that "*I* must have an easy life, *I* must be perfect, and people and conditions should always cater to *me, me, me, me!*"

Why is FI so important in therapy? Because no matter how you originally disturb yourself, when you know you are upset, know your upsetting Beliefs, know what you can probably do about them, and still refuse to work at upsetting yourself, you almost always are a victim of your own FI. For example, if you know that you feel uncomfortable going for job interviews and especially being turned down for a job, and if you realize that you have irrational Beliefs that escalate your discomfort and pain into great anxiety, then you can overcome your anxiety by using REBT to strongly convince yourself that you *can* stand being rejected and that your discomfort is *inconvenient* but hardly *awful*. But you will have to *work* hard at convincing yourself of these sane ideas when you forcefully believe the unsane ones.

You had better, therefore, *use* your knowledge of how to change your ideas that create your anxiety; and you had better *keep working at using it* until you overcome your anxiety and rarely bring it back. You had also better force yourself, no matter how uncomfortable you are, to go on many job interviews until you become less and less panicked about them.

When you indulge in your anxiety instead of making real efforts to overcome it, you are giving in to your FI or discomfort disturbance. And when you temporarily make yourself unanxious but then refuse to keep doing so, you are also indulging in FI.

Low frustration tolerance, then, often leads to anxiety and depression. But even more often it encourages you to maintain your disturbed feelings when you could let them go. To reduce FI, you had better make yourself do many difficult tasks *not pronto*, no matter how you *feel* about doing them.

Do, don't stew! And don't wait until you feel in the mood to do so. Strike while the spirit is cold!

Isn't this Catch-22: To try to overcome your FI—which stems from the idea that working to overcome it *shouldn't* require real effort—by pushing your rump to do "overly" hard things? Yes, it is. But don't forget that Catch-22 stems from an idea in your head and doesn't really exist in itself. And if it is mainly a thought—REBT clearly says—you can overcome it by debating and Disputing it!

The contradiction leading to Catch-22 about FI is:

1. "I shouldn't have to work very hard to get what I want, even though I will benefit in the long run by doing so. It's *too* hard to really work for my own happiness. I need immediate gratification."

2. "The only way to get over my FI and become a long-range, sane hedonist is to work hard to overcome my prejudice against working hard!"

The rational answer that you can use to overcome this paradox is: "Yes, it's quite hard to work to get what I want and to delay immediate gratification in order to derive further pleasure. But it's considerably harder if I don't! Short-range gain will often bring me long-lived pain in the future! Too bad—but that's the way it often is. Sure I have to exert myself to overcome my FI—but I'll require *more* effort, leading to *prolonged* pain, if I don't overcome it."

"Nobody promised me a rose garden. If I insist that they do, I'll only end up with extra thorns!"

Back to REBT's Insight No. 9. Almost always there's no way but work and practice—w-o-r-k and p-r-a-c-t-i-c-e—to eradicate, and to keep away your emotional misery. Insight by itself is not enough. Nor will you get too far by merely acknowledging and expressing your feelings.

You had better *also* challenge and Dispute your irrational Beliefs a thousand times. Arrive at rational Beliefs and forcefully get them into your head a thousand times. Get in touch with, feel, and sometimes express your feelings a thousand times. Act against your disturbed thoughts and emotions a thousand times. And then, if necessary, a thousand more times! For many months, sometimes for years. Sometimes, off and on, for the rest of your life!

We can state Insight No. 9 differently: There is no magical, easy way of changing yourself. Optimism and hope won't do it. Prayer and supplication won't do it. Getting support and love from others won't do it. Even reading this book won't do it! All these things may help you *feel* better. Some of them will show you what to do to *get* better. But in the final analysis, only *you* can make yourself change. You and the persistent *work* you do. Work? Yes, *work*!

You can stop feeling severely anxious, depressed, and otherwise miserable by employing REBT principles of work and practice in two main ways:

1. Use *several* thinking, feeling, and action REBT techniques—such as those explained in this book and other REBT writings. Give each one a fair chance. If one doesn't work, use another, and another, and another! And if one does work, keep trying some of the other REBT techniques, too.

2. Keep using each REBT method many times. Even when one of them—such as singing rational humorous songs to yourself—works beautifully for a while, employ it again and again until you sink its message into your head and into your bones. Overlearn it. And from time to time, keep reviewing it—lest you forget, lest you forget!

Pablo, a forty-year-old travel agent, understood the principles and practice of REBT well and frequently used them with his close friends and with the volunteers at my regular Friday-night Workshop in Problems of Daily Living, to whom he often gave excellent rational suggestions after I interviewed them about their emotional problems. But whenever Pablo became angry at others—which was several times a week—he let his rage boil for over an hour, sometimes for the entire day, before he used REBT to overcome it and allow himself to go back to writing the great American play.

Because of his knowledge of REBT, Pablo knew how he created his fury with irrational Beliefs: "People *shouldn't* act so damned stupidly! What hopeless idiots they are!" And: "My wife, who keeps saying that she loves me, *must not* be so selfish and uncaring! What a rotten hypocrite she is!"

Pablo also often recognized his secondary disturbance and the irrational Beliefs behind it. He knew that he hated *himself* whenever he had a furious outburst at *others*. And he tracked down his self-damning ideas: "I *should* know better than to bring on this childish rage! What a fool I am for not using REBT to eliminate it! How disgusting!"

In spite of his insight into how he kept needlessly enraging and downing himself, Pablo frequently indulged in both these miserable feelings—and kept ruining his playwriting and his relationships. On several occasions, he got into fistfights with "horribly stupid" people. His wife kept leaving him because of his outbursts against her and others. And his plays never got finished. Still he refused to use REBT to overcome his rage and self-hatred.

After many failures to do his REBT homework, Pablo worked out the following plan with his therapy group:

For one month, he would devote at least two hours a day to using—not merely understanding but *using*—REBT. He would especially work at fully accepting himself no matter how many times he foolishly enraged himself against others:

1. He would spend at least ten minutes every day actively Disputing his irrational Beliefs: "I *should* know better than to bring on this foolish rage! What a fool I am for not using REBT to eliminate it! How disgusting!"

2. He would persist at this Disputing until he fully accepted himself *with* his foolish behavior.

3. He would very strongly repeat to himself, at least fifteen times each day, the rational Belief: "Because I am a fallible human, I will often act stupidly and at times *continue* to foolishly enrage myself. Too damned bad!"

4. He would make a list of the disadvantages of damning himself for *anything*, then read and think about this list at least five times each day.

5. He would do at least one REBT shame-attacking exercise daily—force himself to do what he considered a "shameful" or "stupid" act in public (such as singing at the top of his lungs in the subway) and work at *not*—yes, *not*—feeling humiliated or downed when he did it.

6. He would sing to himself several times a day one of the rational humorous songs that rips up perfectionism and self-downing, such as the ones that follow.

PERFECT RATIONALITY
(*Tune:* Luigi Denza, "Funiculi, Funicula")

Some think the world must have a right direction,
    And so do I! And so do I!
Some think that, with the slightest imperfection
    They can't get by—and so do I!

For I, I have to prove I'm superhuman,
     And better far than people are!
To show I have miraculous acumen—
     And always rate among the Great.
Perfect, perfect rationality
     Is, of course, the only thing for me!
How can I ever think of being
     If I must live fallibly?
Rationality must be a perfect thing for me!

BEAUTIFUL HANG-UP
(*Tune:* Stephen Foster, "Beautiful Dreamer")

Beautiful hang-up, why should we part
     When we have shared our whole lives from the start?
We are so used to taking one course
     Oh, what a crime it would be to divorce!
Beautiful hang-up, don't go away!
     Who will befriend me if you do not stay?
Though you still make me look like a jerk,
     Living without you would take so much work!
Living without you would take so much work!

I AM BAD, OH SO BAD!
(*Tune:* Antonin Dvořák, "Going Home," from
The New World Symphony)

I am bad, oh so bad, just a worthless cad!
     Oh, my gad! Let me add: I'm so bad it's sad!
I'm so bad I deserve every ugly twist!
     I'm so bad I've a nerve even to exist!
I'm so bad that I'm clad in pure villainy!
     Oh, I'm so bad, you egad
Must take care of me!
     Yes, take care of me!
Yes, take care of me!

As he worked—and worked and worked!—on his secondary symptom of damning himself for his rage and for not trying hard enough to give up his fury, Pablo also worked on his primary symptom of rage. He took his irrational Beliefs that people *shouldn't* be so stupid and that his wife *must* be less selfish and more caring and (with the help of his therapy group) planned these REBT homework assignments:

1. He spent at least ten minutes a day actively and vigorously Disputing his irrational Beliefs.
2. He forcefully told himself rational coping statements, at least fifteen times a day, such as: "People *should* often act stupidly—because that is their nature!" "My wife *will be* at times selfish and uncaring—and has a perfect right to be more interested in herself than in me!"
3. He penalized himself by burning a hundred-dollar bill every time he got into a fistfight with someone and every time he screamed at his wife.
4. He practiced rational emotive imagery at least once a day by imagining that people were really acting stupidly, letting himself feel very angry about this, and then working on feeling *only* disappointed and frustrated, but *not* angry, about their stupid behavior.
5. He sang to himself every day—and really thought about—several rational humorous songs poking fun at feelings of anger, such as these two popular songs, to which I have put new rational lyrics:

LOVE ME, LOVE ME, ONLY ME!

(Tune: "Yankee Doodle Dandy")
Love me, love me, only me or I will die without you!
Make your love a guarantee, so I can never doubt you!
Love me, love me totally; really, really try, dear;
But if you demand love, too, I'll hate you till I die, dear!

Lyrics by Albert Ellis, copyright © by Albert Ellis Institute

Love me, love me all the time, thoroughly and wholly;
Life turns into slush and slime 'less you love me solely!
Love me with great tenderness, with no ifs or buts, dear.
If you love me somewhat less I'll hate your goddamned
      guts, dear!

GLORY, GLORY HALLELUJAH!
(*Tune:* "Battle Hymn of the Republic")

Mine eyes have seen the glory of relationships that glow
And then falter by the wayside as love passions come—
      and go!
Oh, I've heard of great romances where there is no slightest
      lull—
      But I am skeptical!

Glory, glory hallelujah!
People love ya till they screw ya!
If you'd lessen how they do ya,
      Then don't expect they won't!
Glory, glory hallelujah!
People cheer ya—then pooh-pooh ya!
If you'd soften how they screw ya,
      Then don't expect they won't!

Pablo did a good job of carrying out these thinking, feeling, and activity assignments. And when at times he failed to do his REBT homework, he worked hard at refusing to blame himself for failing. He only criticized his *performance* but not his *self,* his *totality.*

As a result of this REBT homework program, Pablo cut down his temper tantrums to a few times a month. Whenever he did have them, he quickly admitted that he had upset himself and indulged in his rage for only five or ten minutes. Then he found his irrational demands that made him angry and succeeded in actively Disputing and surrendering them in a few minutes. He occasionally slipped and let himself rage for an hour or more. But he usually continued his outbursts for no more than ten minutes—and often for only two or three.

Pablo was happy about the time and energy he saved by his anti-anger program. He no longer wasted hours indulging in his rages and his sulking, and he was able to devote much more time every week to writing his play.

You will find no panacea when you work and practice at changing your self-sabotaging ideas and behaviors. Telling yourself that you *must* work hard at therapy and *have to* keep practicing REBT can even be harmful. And *seeing* how you upset yourself and how you can stop doing so is not enough. *Using* REBT and forcefully *striving* to minimize your misery is the key. Not a magical but a practical key to stubbornly refusing to make yourself miserable about anything. Yes, anything!

REBT Exercise No. 14

For the exercise, you can write out an REBT sheet for Disputing Irrational Beliefs (DIBS). The instructions are given in *A Guide to Rational Living* and in Appendix 3, "Techniques for Disputing Irrational Beliefs," at the end of this book. To do this, take one of your irrational Beliefs (iBs) and ask yourself several important challenging questions about it, until you really give it up and strongly believe—and *feel* that it is false.

The questions that you use in DIBS include the following:

1. What irrational Belief (iB) do I want to Dispute and surrender?
2. Can I rationally prove this Belief?
3. What evidence can I find to disprove this Belief?
4. Does any evidence exist for the truth of this Belief?
5. What are the worst things that could *actually* happen to me if I give up this Belief and act against it?
6. What good things could happen or could I make happen if I give up this Belief?

If you have frustration intolerance about doing REBT and working hard and persistently at it until you begin to change your disturbed thoughts, feelings, and behaviors, you might use this DIBS to change your FI:

1. *What irrational belief (iB) do I want to dispute and surrender?*
   - *Illustrative Answer:* "I must not have to work hard at changing myself with REBT. It should come easy! It's much *too* hard to go to all that trouble. How *awful* that someone won't do it for me!"
2. *Can I rationally prove or support this belief?*
   - *Illustrative Answer:* No.
3. *What evidence can I find to disprove this belief?*
   - *Illustrative Answer:* Considerable evidence, such as:
     a. There is no reason why I *must* not have to work hard at changing myself with REBT. If hard work were not required, changing myself would be very easy. But, obviously, it's not easy! So it looks like I'd better acknowledge that *if* I want to change, I'd damn well better work persistently and hard to do so!
     b. Where is it written that changing myself by using REBT should or ought to come easy? Only in my grandiose wishes and in my silly head! No matter how desirable it is for me to change easily, my desire for ease does not automatically bring it on.
     c. How is it *too* hard for me to go to the trouble of changing myself with REBT? It surely is not *impossibly* hard, though it may be *very* hard. To call it "too hard" is for me to resort to magical thinking, for I really mean that it is harder than I want it to be and therefore it is "too" hard. But this means that I say that whatever I want to be easy must really be easy—that I run the blasted universe! Well, *do* I? Hardly!
     d. Yes, it is hard for me to change by using REBT, but right now it *should be* that hard—for that's the way it is: truly difficult. So it is! Tough! But no matter how tough I find it to be, it *still* is that hard.

e. Yes, it's hard for me to change, but I'd better face the fact that it's much harder if I don't. For then I keep my usual anxiety and depression and probably keep it forever. Look how hard *that* is!

f. Where is the evidence that it is *awful* if someone doesn't make me easily change or do my REBT for me and thus make me change! It's not *awful*, because *awful*, in the sense I'm using it, means *more than* bad; it may be bad, or inconvenient, that I have to work at the REBT to change myself, but that inconvenience is hardly 101 percent or 120 percent bad. Not even 99 percent. And the badder I see it, the more exaggerated badness that I give to it, the *more* frustrated I'll feel and the more I'll interfere with my using REBT to change myself. So I'd better see it as *just* bad or inconvenient.

4. ***Does any evidence exist for the truth of my irrational belief, "I must not have to work hard at changing myself with REBT?"***

   • *Illustrative Answer:* "None that I can see. There is a good deal of evidence that it *is* hard to work at changing myself with REBT and that it right now *should* be hard (because it realistically is!). But although it would be very fortunate if I could easily and quickly change, just by knowing REBT and thinking about how good it is, that kind of good fortune just doesn't exist in the world. If I *presently* work hard at using REBT, I may *later* find it easy and automatic to do so. But at the present time it's hard because it's hard! So, having no better resource, I'd better do the work it entails gracefully, without creating for myself an even *bigger* hassle about it!

5. ***What are the worst things that could actually happen to me if I give up the belief that it's too hard to work at changing myself with REBT?***

   • *Illustrative Answer:*

     a. I would keep working at REBT and that would be a real pain in the neck. So it would be a pain in the neck! But if

I don't work at it, I would continue to have all the hassles and troubles I do have—and I would presumably have them forever!

b. IF I don't use REBT and don't work at it to get over my problems, they will not only remain, but they will most probably increase. That will be even worse. But even if I do nothing and my problems increase, it will *only* be uncomfortable and inconvenient. It still will not be *awful*—that is, badder than it *should* be, and *totally* bad. It will only be bad!

c. If I work at REBT, the worst that could really happen would be that I still won't improve at all, so all my work would therefore be wasted. But at least I would then know that I had *tried* to do my best to get better. That way, without working and without trying, I will never even know how much better I could get—or could not get. So I had better make the effort and see how well I can do.

d. Even if I work hard at REBT and never get better at all, I could then still live with my frustration and my pain. This is unlikely—for if I work I most likely will improve to some degree. But if I never improve one bit, I don't. Whatever happens—or does not happen—to me in life is *still* only a bother, still only an inconvenience. And if I stop whining and screaming *about* that inconvenience, that in itself will save me gratuitous, *extra* bothering of myself. So I'd still better do the work.

6. **What good things might happen or might I make happen if I work at using REBT in regard to my problems?**
   • *Illustrative Answer:*
   a. I might really get over my problem by using REBT. I'm now anxious and depressed, and by using REBT I could well become considerably less anxious and depressed. Or even *un*anxious and *un*depressed!
   b. If I overcome my low frustration tolerance in this area I will tend to become more generally disciplined and may

well overcome my FI in various other areas of my life, such as overeating and procrastination.

c. It is a great challenge for me to enjoy life while working hard to use REBT and while giving up present pleasures for future gains. The challenge of not upsetting myself while I am going through some amount of deprivation is one of the best challenges that I can take in life.

d. By working against my frustration intolerance, even if it takes me a while to succeed, I will get better and better at it, can at times *enjoy* my activity, and can see that I am increasingly promoting my *own* independence and emotional mastery. What could be more rewarding than running my *own* life?

15

REBT Insight No. 10: Forcefully Changing Your Beliefs, Feelings, and Behaviors

You can express thoughts, feelings, and behaviors lightly or strongly, mildly or forcefully—as you can easily observe. You can feel mildly or intensely sad about a loss. You can exercise vigorously or gently. You can be greatly or moderately addicted to smoking or over-eating.

Can thoughts, too, be weak or strong?

Robert Abelson, Robert Zajonc, and other psychologists say yes. As Abelson pointed out a number of years ago, you can have "cool" and "hot" cognitions. According to REBT, your "hot" thoughts influence you more and create more intense feelings than do your "cool" thoughts.

Thus, if you have to pass an exam to get a job, you may have a cool thought: "Jobs like this frequently require a test." Your cool, descriptive thought will lead to your having little or no feeling.

You may also have a warm or preferential thought—which in REBT we call a rational Belief—about the test and the job: "I definitely want to pass this test and get this job, and since the test doesn't seem too hard, I like taking it." This warm thought will probably lead you to feel optimistic and help you do well on the test.

You may finally have a hot or highly evaluative thought: "I *have* to pass this test and get this job in order to enjoy life at all and to accept myself as a good person! If the test is harder than it seems and I fail it, that would be *awful* and would prove that I'm a schnook who will never get a decent job!" This is a hot thought—an irrational Belief in REBT—and will likely make you feel intense anxiety and interfere with your doing well on the test.

REBT also states that you hold some hot thoughts strongly, rigidly, and forcefully, while you hold some lightly and less vividly. You may believe that you must pass a test and are a real clod if you don't and may believe this (a) occasionally or always, (b) loosely or devoutly, (c) mildly or intensely, (d) blandly or vividly, (e) softly or loudly, or (f) in a limited way (about one situation) or generally (about many situations).

As you can see, your hot thoughts include many kinds of heat! REBT also holds that you create more intense feelings—and particularly disturbed feelings—with your hot than with your warm thoughts. Hot thinking often encourages you to have self-defeating emotions and behaviors that persist longer and are harder for you to change.

If you fanatically believe that you must *always* pass important tests and get *every single* job for which you apply, and you also believe that you are a *hopeless nincompoop* when you *in any way* fail, you will tend to make yourself extremely anxious when you go for a test or a job interview. This anxiety may disrupt your whole life, and you will have one heck of a time relieving it. Moreover, you will often feel such intense panic and discomfort that you may well make yourself terrified about it. You then bring on strong secondary symptoms of anxiety about your anxiety.

Because your hot thoughts create intense and lasting anxiety and depression, you had better acquire Insight No. 10: *If you mildly Dispute your irrational Beliefs (iBs) you may not change them and keep them changed. Therefore, you had better powerfully and persistently argue against them and persuade yourself that they are false.*

When, for example, you ask yourself—at point D, Disputing of your iBs—"Why *must* I always pass important tests?" you had better very vigorously (and *often*) reply: "I *don't* have to do so! I'd love to pass and will work hard to do so. But if I don't, I don't! I definitely *want* this job, but I never, never *need* it. I *can* be happy if I don't get it, though not *as* happy as if I do. I *can* pass other tests and get other jobs even if I fail at getting this one. I will only be a *person who* failed this time, and clearly not a *hopeless failure!*"

REBT says that the more emphatically and the more frequently you challenge and debate your red-hot negative thoughts, the quicker and more completely you will kill them—and the more you will re-duce (and *keep* away) the disturbed feelings they create.

So back to Insight No. 10: When you track down your iBs that make you anxious (and that panic you *about* your anxiety), you can become a *passionate* scientist who strongly comes up with rational answers to your irrational Beliefs.

Take Tom, for example. Although tall and handsome, aged thirty-five, and a successful physician, he kept falling madly in love with fine women—and quickly turned them all off. They found him too insecure, too needy. As I often ask my clients, who *needs* a needy person? Not Tom's women friends!

Tom understood REBT and knew exactly what he was telling himself to make himself shaky when he met a charming woman: "I love her so strongly and would feel so deprived if she did not return my feelings that I *absolutely must* win her. I *have to*! I've *got to*! I *must!*"

Noting this kind of *must*urbation and seeing that it didn't work, Tom used REBT to try to give it up, and kept asking himself, "Why *must* I win this woman I care for? Do I really *have to* please her? Would I *die* without her love?"

He gave the correct, rational answers to these Disputations and helped himself somewhat. For a while. But then he fell right back to his great need. And to his insecurity.

I gave Tom the REBT homework assignment of having a *forceful* rational dialogue with himself and recording the dialogue. He tried to do so and brought me in a cassette tape in which he nicely Disputed his iBs about winning the love of a special woman, but when I and members of his therapy group listened to it, we found his arguments good—but his tone wishy-washy. He *knew* the rational words to combat his neediness; but he obviously didn't *believe* them.

So I had Tom do the tape over, asking him to be much *harder* on his irrational Beliefs.

No dice. His second tape dialogue was only a bit stronger in tone than his first one. And he still remained a love slob.

His third tape was much better. Part of it went as follows:

Tom's irrational voice: If Cora, who's just about the best woman I have met in years, doesn't really love me, what decent woman will? None!

Tom's rational voice: None? What crap! With so many fine women I could meet? Obviously, *some* would care for me. Even if they were stupid for doing so!

Tom's irrational voice: But suppose they only cared because they were stupid. That would show what an unlovable jerk I am!

Tom's rational voice: To hell it would! At worst, it would show that I am sadly lacking some good traits. But never that I am totally unlovable. Nor would it show, if no woman found me desirable, that I would be a *complete jerk*. I would just be a loser in *that* area.

Tom's irrational voice: Yes, the most important of *all* areas. That would really make you one damned loser!

Tom's rational voice: No—a loser in *love*. But not in *every* area. Not in *life*! A loser to fine women. But not, dammit, to me!

Tom's irrational voice: There you go—rationalizing again! What good is your life if you can't have real love? So you'll be a great physician. Hah!

Tom's rational voice: Yes—I hope—a great physician. And great at sports! And a fine reader! I have lots of things I can really enjoy—even if I never find a good partner.

Tom's irrational voice: Never? Never?

Tom's rational voice: Yes, never! Immanuel Kant never mated—or probably ever even dated. And he had a good life! Many other outstanding people, too, were happy without love. But whether they were or not, *I'm* going to be! Just as soon as I stop whining about my being "unlovable"!

As soon as Tom learned the knack of *vigorously, powerfully* Disputing his own irrational Beliefs—which he now referred to as his Bullshit—he began to do so many times. I and the members of his therapy group didn't have to tell him, after he recorded a dialogue like the one above, that it was strong enough. His *feeling* of immense relief from anxiety and depression showed him that it was. He *immediately* felt he didn't *need* (though he still keenly *desired*) love. And he felt that way for the next few weeks.

As Tom kept fiercely arguing himself out of being a love slob, he felt much less needy. Four months later, he was almost totally improved—and consequently the women he dated often wanted to continue seeing him—and some highly desirable ones tried to cart him off to the altar! A year later he began to live with the one he liked best, and three years later he married her. He is now teaching her how to actively—and quite vigorously—talk herself out of some of her own emotional Bullshit.

REBT Exercise No. 15

Take one of your irrational Beliefs that you really want to give up, because you know that you are seriously defeating yourself by holding it, and dispute it both mildly and moderately, on the one hand, and vigorously or powerfully on the other hand. You may do this by writing out the irrational Belief and then making one column of mild disputings and changing of it, and one column of vigorous disputings and changing. Or better yet, you can record your irrational Belief on an audio recorder, and then have a dialogue with yourself on the recorder, in the course of which you moderately *and* powerfully dispute this Belief until you really feel that you have made some real progress in giving up and changing it to a set of strong rational philosophies.

A sample of your written out Disputing might go as follows:

IRRATIONAL BELIEF

I really have to pass this test that I am about to take because if I don't, my whole career will go down the drain and I'll surely end up working all my life in some menial capacity and making very little money, and that would be absolutely horrible! What a worm I would then be!

Instead of, or in addition to, disputing your irrational Belief powerfully and vigorously on paper (as in the above illustration), you can have both a mild and a forceful dialogue with yourself on a tape recorder, and make sure that you end up by believing and feeling the forceful arguments that you present on the tape. Take this self-dialogue, for example:

Mild Disputing and Rational Answer	*Powerful Disputing and Rational Answer*
If I fail this test I can take other tests and pass them later. So why worry?	Even if I fail the test and every other test, I still can get a good job doing something. And if I don't, I don't! I can still be happy.
My whole career won't go down the drain. I'll just be slower at getting what I want in the course of it.	If my whole damned career went down the drain, I could still get another enjoyable and well-paying career!
I'll sooner or later probably pass this test and get some kind of a decent career.	I'll darned well pass this test one of these days, probably this time! And whether or not I do, I'm absolutely determined to get a good career!
If I keep working in a menial capacity, it won't kill me.	Whatever capacity I keep working in, I am determined to get some very good things out of the work. And even if I never do enjoy it, I can always find other aspects of my life that will be exceptionally enjoyable!

Mild Disputing and Rational Answer

Powerful Disputing and Rational Answer

If I make very little money all my life, I can still get by.

If I make very little money all my life, I cannot only get by but somehow manage to have a damned good time. Money is important but it clearly isn't everything!

It would be pretty inconvenient to make little money all my life, but it wouldn't be the end of the world.

It would be damned inconvenient to make little money all my life, but in one way or another I will work my butt off to make more. If somehow I don't succeed, I will merely reduce my expenses and be one of the happiest people alive who lives on very little!

If I fail this test and make less money for the rest of my life, I'll only be a person who failed but not a rotten worm.

No matter how many tests I fail or how little money I make in life, I am never a worm or a totally incompetent person. I am and will always be a fallible human, but I can always fully accept myself and look for every possible pleasure in life no matter how badly I act in certain respects. I am I; just because I am alive and am myself I ALWAYS deserve to have the best time I can have during my lifetime. Now how the hell do I manage to have that good time? By striving for it!

IRRATIONAL BELIEF

My friend, Norbert, borrowed money from me and said that he'd pay it back quickly. Now several months have gone by and he still hasn't paid it. What is more, he's acting as if I just gave him the money as a gift and that he's not supposed to pay it back. If he gets a lot of money, he says, he will give me back what I lent him, but just out of the goodness of his heart and not because he really owes it to me. How could he do a thing like that to me?! What a thorough bastard he is! This means that he has no real good qualities. He deserves to be severely damned and punished, and I think I'll really get back at him. I'll show him that he can't act that way to me!

ILLUSTRATIVE DIALOGUE

Irrational you: How could he do a thing like that?

Mild answer: He just could. That's the way he often behaves just like that. Well, that's his problem.

Strong answer: He damned well easily could do a thing like that! It's not the first time he's acted that way, and I'll bet it won't be the last! I wish to hell that he wouldn't be like that, but he often is. Tough! But I expect it—and take it!

Irrational you: But after all I did for him! I went out of my way to lend him the money and he *still* insists that I gave it to him! What a thorough bastard he is!

Mild answer: Yes, I really went out of my way to lend him the money, but that doesn't mean that he has to go out of his way to pay me back. He's not a thorough bastard—though he sometimes acts in a bastardly manner.

Strong answer: Yes, I went out of my way to lend him the money, but that never in the least means that he has to go out of his way, or to be very honest, and to pay me back. Whatever I decide to do is *me*; and what he decides to do is *Norbert*. Well, that certainly is a rotten thing for him to do, and I definitely won't trust him in the future—or lend him any *more* money! But he's not a thorough bastard—not even an *un*thorough bastard. He's just a fallible human, like all of us are, and this is one of his great fallibilities. Well, I'll never like his having this kind of failing, but I can clearly live with it, still try to get my money back, and be a happy human—though not *as* happy—if I never get it. Isn't it too darned bad that some of my best "friends" turn out to be unfriendly?

Irrational you: I still think he's a thorough bastard! If he can do a thing like this, he has no real good qualities.

Mild answer: Isn't that an exaggeration on my part? Of course, he, like all humans, has *some* good qualities. It's just this aspect of him that is bad.

Strong answer: What nonsense! Of course he has good qualities, too. Everyone does. Even Hitler doubtless had a few. But for all his good qualities—and I'd better admit that at other times he has been quite good to me—his not accepting that he borrowed the money and falsely claiming that I gave it to him is really a bad *act*. And that's just what I'm going to try to show him—not that *he* is bad but that his dishonest *act* is. I'm really going to persist at trying to show him that. But if I can't, I can't. At worst, I'll just lose the money and cut him off as a friend.

Irrational you: Damned well I'll cut him off as a friend! Me, friendly with a person like that? Never! He deserves to be severely damned and punished, and I think I'll really get back at him.

Mild answer: What's the use of getting back at him? I'll only waste more time doing that. I might as well drop it. But he really is a pretty crummy person.

Strong answer: How silly of me to try to get back at him! I wasted enough time and money already in dealing with him, and now I'm just going to continue this nonsense by thinking about him and wasting time and energy trying to get back at him. He may theoretically deserve, in a thoroughly just world, to be penalized for his bad behavior to me, but he hardly deserves to be severely damned and punished. No human is subhuman; no human is damnable. If I foolishly stole from him, the universe wouldn't spy on me and command that I must be damned and punished. Why, then, should he be? I'll still try to put pressure on him, but not angry pressure, to get my money back. But no waste of time damning him!

Irrational you: No matter how much time and energy it takes, I'll show him that he can't act that way to me. I'll fix his wagon! And while I'm at it, maybe there's something I can do to get back at his wife and family, too!

Mild answer: There's no way that I can certainly show him that he *can't* act that way to me. He has a right, as a human, to do whatever he wishes, even when he's clearly wrong. I'd better drop the whole thing and forget it.

Strong answer: Of course, he *can* act that way to me. Damned well he can! In fact, he has a great talent for acting in that unfriendly way, and now that I've discovered this I'd better accept that grim reality. And I have no way, probably, of showing him that he can't act that way to me. No matter how vindictive I become, and even hurt his wife and family, that won't show him. In fact, it will probably show him, in his eyes, what a "louse" I am, and then he'll deliberately not pay the money back to me—and perhaps vindictively try to hurt me and my family. If I foolishly try to fix his wagon, I'll very likely fix my own wagon in the process. Then I'll suffer even *more* than I'm now suffering. What crap on my part! Just because he's wrong doesn't mean that I have to spend the rest of my life vindictively being wrong, too. Let me just try to talk to him, without anger and vindictiveness again, and see what I can do. And if I can't do anything, well, I just can't! I'd better still drop it. Yes, drop it and go about my own business!

When you have written out or done an audio recording on forcefully debating and disputing your irrational Belief about something, go over it to make it even stronger. Let some of your friends or associates go over it with you. Work on being strong but not violent. Try not to perpetuate the craziness in which you are engaging or that is being destructively used against you. Practice strongly—yes, s-t-r-o-n-g-l-y—disputing your own nutty ideas!

16

REBT Insight No. 11: Achieving
Emotional Change Is Not Enough—
Maintaining It Is Harder!

As Mark Twain said: "It's easy to quit smoking. I've done it a thousand times."

This sums up the history of dieting, too. For every hundred people who lose thirty pounds or more by various diets, well over 90 percent gain all or most of it back.

Similarly with psychotherapy. Millions of people change by going for therapy. But almost all of them at times fall back. For a while, their feelings of anxiety, depression, and rage disappear. And then return!

Sometimes, if you work at erasing your emotional misery, you take two steps forward—and only one step backward. Sometimes the reverse. Sometimes you completely free yourself of depression. Then you fall right back in the thick black soup again. You may never again experience an old problem—such as a fear of public speaking. But then you bring on an entirely new one—such as fear of job hunting.

This brings us to Insight No. 11: *You may for a while find it easy to change your feelings. But you'd better keep working, working, working to maintain your gains.*

Almost no person gets completely or forever cured of misery. Including you!

What can you do, then, to maintain your improvement and to deal with backsliding?

A great deal.

At the Albert Ellis Institute in New York City, we have given much thought to this question and have come up with a pamphlet that we give to all our clients. Let me demonstrate Insight No. 11 of REBT by showing you some of the main points in "How to Maintain and Enhance Your Rational Emotive Behavior Therapy Gains." You'll find it in Appendix 2 of this book.

What are important things you can remember to maintain your improvement?

1. When you fall back to old feelings of anxiety, depression, or self-downing, zero in on the exact thoughts, feelings, and behaviors you once changed to make yourself improve. If you again feel depressed, think back to how you previously used REBT to make yourself undepressed. For example, you may remember that:
   a. You stopped telling yourself that you were worthless and that you couldn't ever succeed in getting what you wanted.
   b. You did well in a job and proved to yourself that you did have some ability to succeed.
   c. You forced yourself to go on interviews instead of avoiding them and thereby overcame your anxiety about them.
      Remind yourself of thoughts, feelings, and behaviors that you have changed and that you have helped yourself by changing.
2. Keep thinking, thinking, and thinking rational Beliefs (rBs) or coping statements, such as: "It's great to succeed but I can fully accept myself as a person and enjoy life considerably even when I fail!" Don't merely parrot these statements but carefully *think* them many times. Yes, *strongly* think them through until you truly begin to feel that they are true.

3. Keep looking for, discovering, and disputing your irrational Beliefs (iBs) with which you are once again upsetting yourself. Take each important irrational Belief—such as, "I *have to* succeed in order to be a worthwhile person!"—and keep asking yourself: "Why is this belief true?" "Where is the evidence that my worth as a person depends on my succeeding?" "In what way would I be a rotten human if I failed at an important task?"

    Keep forcefully disputing your irrational Beliefs whenever you see that you are letting them creep back in again. And even when you are not bothering yourself, realize that you may bring them back. So ask yourself what you think they are, make yourself fully conscious of them—and vigorously dispute them.

4. Keep taking risks and doing things that you irrationally fear—such as riding in elevators, socializing, job hunting, or creative writing. As you are overcoming one of your irrational fears, keep thinking *and* acting against it on a regular basis. *Do* what you are afraid to do—and very often!

    If you feel uncomfortable when you force yourself to do things you irrationally fear, to hell with the discomfort! Don't allow yourself to cop out—and thereby to preserve your fears forever! Often, make yourself as uncomfortable as you can be, in order to erase your fears and to become unanxious and comfortable later.

5. Learn to clearly see the difference between healthy bad feelings—such as those of sorrow, regret, and frustration—when you do not get some of the important things you want, and unhealthy bad feelings—such as those of depression, anxiety, self-hatred, and self-pity—when you are deprived. Whenever you feel *over*concerned (panicked) or *needlessly* miserable (depressed), admit that you are having a very common but an unhealthy feeling and that you are bringing it on yourself with some dogmatic *shoulds*, *oughts*, or *musts*.

    Realize that you are quite capable of changing your unhealthy (or *must*urbatory) feelings back into healthy (or preferential) ones. Get in touch with your depressed feelings and work on them until you *only* feel sorry and regretful. Get in touch with your anxious feelings and work on them until you *only* feel concerned and vigilant.

Use rational emotive imagery to vividly imagine unpleasant Activating Events even before they happen. Let yourself feel unhealthily upset (anxious, depressed, enraged, or self-downing) as you imagine them. Then work on your feelings to change them to healthy emotions (concern, sorrow, annoyance, or regret) as you keep imagining some of the worst things happening. Don't give up until you actually do change your feelings.

6. Avoid procrastination. Do unpleasant tasks fast—today! If you still procrastinate, reward yourself with certain things that you enjoy—for example, eating, vacationing, reading, or socializing—only *after* you have performed the tasks that you easily avoid. If this won't work, give yourself a severe penalty—such as talking to a boring person for two hours or burning a hundred dollar bill—every time that you procrastinate.

7. Make an absorbing *challenge* and an *adventure* out of maintaining your emotional health and keeping yourself reasonably happy no matter what kind of misfortunes assail you. Make the removal of your misery one of the most important things in your life—something you are utterly determined to achieve. Fully acknowledge that you always have some *choice* about how to think, feel, and behave; throw yourself actively into making that choice for yourself.

8. Remember—and use—the three main insights of REBT that were first outlined in *Reason and Emotion in Psychotherapy* in 1962:

Insight No. 1: You largely *choose* to disturb yourself about the "upsetting" events of your life. You mainly *feel* the way you *think*. When obnoxious and frustrating things happen to you at point A (Activating Events), you consciously or unconsciously *select* rational Beliefs (rBs) that lead you to feel sad and regretful and you also *select* irrational Beliefs (iBs) that lead you to feel anxious, depressed, and self-hating.

Insight No. 2: No matter how or when you acquired your irrational Beliefs and habits, you now, in the present, *choose* to maintain them—and that is why you are *now* disturbed. Poor conditions (in the past and present) *affect* you, but they don't *disturb* you. Your present *philosophy* creates your *current* disturbance.

Insight No. 3: There is no magical way for you to change your personality and your strong tendencies to upset yourself. You really change with *work and practice. Your* work and *your* practice.

9. Keep looking—steadily but unfrantically—for personal pleasures and enjoyments—such as reading, entertainment, sports, hobbies, art, science, and other vital absorbing interests. Make your major life goal the achievement of emotional health—and also that of real enjoyment.

   Try to become involved in a long-term purpose, goal, or interest in which you can remain truly absorbed. *Make* yourself a good, happy life by giving yourself something to live *for.* In that way you will distract yourself from serious woes and will help preserve your mental health.

10. Keep in touch with several other people who know something about REBT and who can help review it with you. Tell them about your problems and let them know how you are using REBT to overcome them. See if they agree with your solutions and can suggest additional REBT methods to work against your irrational Beliefs.

11. Practice using REBT with some of your friends and associates who will let you try to help them with it. The more often you use it with others, and try to talk them out of their self-defeating ideas, the more you will understand the main principles of REBT and be able to use them with yourself.

   When you see other people acting irrational and upset, try to figure out—with or without talking to them about it—

their main irrational Beliefs and how these can be actively and vigorously disputed. This, again, gives you practice in working on your own iBs.

12. Keep reading REBT writings and listening to REBT audio- and audio-visual recordings. Read and listen to several of these—particularly my books, *Humanistic Psychotherapy; A Guide to Personal Happiness; A Guide to Rational Living; Feeling Better, Getting Better, and Staying Better;* and *Overcoming Procrastination,* as well as Paul Hauck's *Overcoming the Rating Game* and Howard Young's *A Rational Counseling Primer.*

Keep going back to this REBT material to remind yourself of some of the main rational emotive behavior philosophies.

Georgiana, a thirty-four-year-old bookkeeper, came to REBT because she was intensely jealous and angry when her husband, David, kept staring at attractive young women whenever they went out together. He denied doing this, but she insisted that he did and was convinced (to her horror) that every time he had sex with her he was imagining some woman with enormous breasts (Georgiana had small ones) that he had been staring at that day.

She became so upset about this that she often stopped having intercourse with him just before the two of them were about to come to orgasm. This "drives me up the wall," he said. And although he loved and liked her, he was just about ready to leave.

Georgiana saw me for several sessions of individual REBT and then joined one of my regular therapy groups for eight months. She realized that she was absolutistically demanding that David lust after only her and never even think of another woman. She also saw that even if he did at times stare at other women and think of them while having sex with her, that meant nothing about her own looks or sexiness. So she became only moderately jealous of David's interest in other women.

A few months later, however, Georgiana again became extremely jealous and insecure. So, as a homework assignment that she worked out with her therapy group, she spent several weeks reviewing and working on some of the points listed in the previous chapter of this book:

1. She reminded herself that one of the best means of overcoming her jealousy was refusing to connect her worth as a person with her *ability* to satisfy David sexually. She showed herself many times that she could accept herself fully even if she no longer greatly aroused him.

2. She forcefully kept telling herself the rational Belief (rB): "I *can* be loved by David and have a good marriage even if he *does* lust after women with big busts!"

3. She kept challenging and Disputing her irrational Belief (iB): "I *must* be the only truly exciting woman to David!"

4. She deliberately kept going with David to restaurants and other places where he was likely to see attractive women. She *assumed* he was staring at them and kept telling herself, "Tough!—that's the way he is: desiring other women. I can live with it!"

5. She saw the difference between her feeling *healthily* sorry and *unhealthily* panicked and depressed when David stared at other women. She used rational-emotive imagery, imagined him eagerly staring, and made herself feel *only* sorry and disappointed, but *not* anxious and self-downing.

6. She noticed that she was making excuses for not viewing the Miss America beauty contest on TV. So she set herself a penalty of burning a ten-dollar bill for every minute she avoided viewing it with David. She saw the entire contest and burned no money.

7. She gave herself the challenge of not only refusing to be miserable but actually enjoying her outings with David, even when she was sure he was staring at women with big breasts.

8. She repeated REBT's original Insights No. 1, 2, and 3 to herself, especially No. 3: "Becoming less jealous requires *work and practice*. So I damned well had better keep working and working against my silly jealousy!"

9. She absorbed herself in the vital interest of designing and making her own clothes. She kept focusing on how well *they* looked rather than on how puny and "ugly" were her breasts.

10. She talked to a few of the group members and to her women friends who also knew REBT and who kept helping her go back to using it when she slipped into jealous rages.

11. She used REBT to help her friends and business associates (including her supervisor), and thus taught it better to herself.

12. She recorded her part of her group sessions and listened several times a week to the Disputing and advice that I and the other members used with her. She kept reading REBT books and pamphlets, even though she had previously read them several times. She thereby kept reminding herself on points that she had half forgotten.

As a result of applying herself so strongly to REBT maintenance practices, Georgiana got to the point where she rarely felt intense jealousy and rage. She was able, with the group's full consent, to quit therapy and keep working on her problem successfully by herself. She and her husband still come from time to time to my regular Friday night live demonstrations of REBT. Her husband is most enthusiastic about her progress and has come to see one of our other therapists at the Albert Ellis Institute in New York to work on his anxiety about his job.

REBT Exercise No. 16

Select some task that you would like to do and know that you preferably should do but you are avoiding or—at very best—are procrastinating on and therefore doing very slowly. For example:

Finishing a paper or a report

Checking your monthly bank statement

Doing your REBT homework

Making business calls, on the phone or in person

Coming to work regularly on time

Writing a new job résumé

Answering a long overdue letter to a friend

Outlining a book you want to write

Preparing to give a talk or a workshop

Look for the things you are telling yourself to make yourself avoid or procrastinate. Especially:

Shoulds and musts: "I *shouldn't* have to do this difficult paper." "My REBT homework *must* be easy to do."

Awfulizings: "It's *awful* to check this damned bank statement!" "It's *terrible* to make these blasted telephone calls!"

I-can't-stand-it-itis: "I *can't stand* dressing to go to this party! I *can't bear* stupid parties like this one is sure to be!"

Too-hards: "It's not only too hard to write this outline for a book, it's *too* hard! It's harder than it *should be*!"

Self-damning: "Because I'm not preparing this speech, as I *should* be, and because others prepare their speeches with no delays, there's something basically wrong with me, and that makes me an *incompetent person*. What a total idiot I am!"

Always and neverness: "Since I fell back at doing my REBT, as I *must* not do, I'll *always* be no good at doing it and will *never* do it well."

Hopelessness: "Because I've been late to work a hundred times, as I *must* not be, it's *hopeless*, and I simply *can't* make myself be on time!"

Select some behavior or habit in which you are foolishly indulging even though you are harming yourself considerably by continuing to indulge in it. For example:

Smoking cigarettes

Overeating

Telling yourself what a rotten person you are

Drinking too much

Overspending

Doing pleasant tasks, like television viewing, instead of working on your REBT homework

Continuing to make yourself enraged at people's stupidities and inefficiencies

Indulging in foolish phobias (such as avoiding using escalators or elevators)

Look for the things you are telling yourself to pander to immediate gratification and to make yourself addicted to harmful habits. Especially:

Shoulds and musts: "Even though it's doing me great harm, I *must* have the relief of smoking this cigarette right now. I *absolutely need it* to relieve my tension."

Awfulizings: "It's *awful* that I just can't enjoy myself instead of working steadily at changing myself with REBT! It's *terrible* that I must go through present pain to get later gain!"

I-can't-stand-it-itis: "I *can't stand* pushing away this delicious food when it tastes so good! I need this extra food right now!"

Too-hards: "It's not merely hard for me to give up the pleasure and relaxation of booze and marijuana, it's much *too* hard! It *must* not be that hard!"

Self-damnings: "Because I'm not working my butt off at doing REBT as I *ought* to be doing, and because I'm indulging instead in immediate enjoyable activities, as I *ought not* be doing, I'm a *pretty rotten* person who *deserves* to keep suffering."

Always and neverness: "Because I keep spending money on things I really do not need to get short-term pleasures that I foolishly think that I do need, I'll *never* change and will *always* be a stupid spendthrift!"

Hopelessness: "Because I have fallen back several times from doing my REBT homework, and instead have taken the easier and instantly more gratifying path of not working at changing myself, it's *hopeless*. I *can't* stop indulging in easy things, so I might as well give in to my natural tendencies and forget about changing myself."

Once you look for and discover your irrational Beliefs (iBs) with which you are creating your frustration intolerance and your indulgences, actively and vigorously dispute all your shoulds, oughts, musts, your awfulizings, your I-can't-stand-its, your too-hards, your self-damnings, your always and neverousnesses, and your conclusions of hopelessness. For example:

Disputing: "Why *must* my REBT homework be easy to do? Why *shouldn't* I have a hard time doing it and continuing to do it?"

Answer: "There's no reason why it should be easy, and several reasons why it should be hard: (a) Because it *is* hard. (b) Because I'm not yet used to doing it, and it may well become easier as I *continue* to do so. (c) Because it's natural for me to act foolishly, and at times highly *un*natural for me to act sensibly. So I'd better keep acting well, until I make it more 'natural.' "

Disputing: "What makes it *awful* to keep checking my damned bank account?"

Answer: "Nothing makes it *awful*, since it's only, in itself, a real nuisance. Only *I* make it *awful*—by foolishly *defining* it in this way. So I'd better stop that nonsense and *only* see it as it actually is—a required pain in the neck!"

Disputing: "Where is the evidence that it's *too* hard for me to give up the pleasure and relaxation of booze and marijuana? Prove that it *must* not be that hard!"

Answer: "If it were really *too* hard, then I couldn't possibly give up this pleasure at all. But of course I can give it up—if I *accept*, without childishly whining about and immensely exaggerating, its difficulty. Apparently it isn't *too* hard for me to whine and moan about it. Only too easy! So I'd better stop *making* it harder than it really is by having a temper tantrum about it. So it's hard! Tough! But it's not *horrible!*"

Disputing: "Even if I never prepare this speech, and even if I find that other people easily and quickly prepare their speeches, how does that wrong behavior of mine, procrastination, make me a thoroughly *incompetent person?*"

Answer: "It doesn't, of course. It makes me a person who is not acting competently, right now, in this particular way, and who still has the ability—if I push myself!—to act more competently in the future. If I were a thoroughly incompetent person, I could do practically nothing well. And that of course is quite false: since I do many things with no trouble at all. So I'd better focus on this incompetent *act*, and not on my 'inadequate personhood.' Yes, I'm still fallible and will most probably always be. Now how do I stop this procrastinating and make myself *less* fallible? Once again: by prodding—yes, prodding!—myself."

Disputing: "Even though I keep spending money on things I really do not need in order to get short-term pleasure that I foolishly think that I do need, how does that indicate that I'll *never* change and will *always* be a stupid spendthrift?"

Answer: "It doesn't! No matter how many times I idiotically overspend, I can most likely change and stop it now and in the future. If my past mistakes proved that I will *never* be able to undo them, I could never have learned the multiplication table! They only prove that I easily and often fail—as just about all humans do. But not *always*! And not that I'm doomed to *never* succeed!"

Disputing: "Let me acknowledge that I have fallen back several times from doing my REBT homework, and instead have taken the easier and instantly more gratifying path of not working at changing myself. Where is it written that this makes things *hopeless* and that I *can't* stop indulging in easy things? How does this prove that I might as well give in to my natural tendencies to take things easily and that I should forget about changing myself?"

Answer: "It doesn't! Just because I have natural tendencies to take things easily, and just because I therefore keep falling back from doing my REBT homework, I'd better work harder to keep doing and doing this homework, until I acquire a 'second nature' and begin to automatically and fairly easily do it. No matter how difficult it is to do something, or to not give in to any of my compulsions, that never proves that it's *hopeless* and that I *can't* change. Even when something is *next* to impossible, it usually can eventually be done. Fortunately, I *made myself* this way, even though I had great help from my heredity and my environment! And that means that, in all probability, with persistent effort I can make myself act another, better way!"

Keep observing and admitting your backsliding at REBT or at anything else, and keep noticing how often and how nicely you are addicted to striving for some kind of immediate gratification rather than for long-range gain and happiness. Stubbornly refuse to put yourself down for your frustration intolerance, and then keep working to eliminate it. With actual addictive, compulsive, and indulgent behaviors, force yourself many times to stop them. And when you later fall back—as you often may—to indulging in them again, force yourself, no matter how hard it is, to give them up, give them up, give them up.

Because virtually all harmful habits that you favor award you some kind of quick pleasure or payoff, use the principles of reward, reinforcement, or what B. F. Skinner calls operant conditioning (and what other psychologists often call contingency management) to help you give them up. When you contingently reinforce yourself, you pick some action or behavior that is pleasurable, and preferably even *more* pleasurable than the habit you are trying to give up, and you allow yourself this pleasure AFTER you have refused to engage in the habit you are trying to break.

Suppose, for example, you want to stop smoking cigarettes or want to eat no more than 1,500 calories a day. You look for some pleasure that you find most enjoyable and that you tend to engage in every day in the week—such as listening to music, reading the newspaper, masturbating or having some other kind of sex, having social conversations, exercising, or television viewing. You then allow yourself to have this great pleasure only AFTER you have refrained from smoking or AFTER you have stopped before eating 1,501 calories. Be very strict about this reinforcement or reward, or it will not work. No excuses! If you have a single cigarette or eat even fifty extra calories, no music, no newspaper reading, no television viewing, or no other reward that you have set for yourself. Right!—none!

Stiff penalties are even better, if you will properly use them. For you obviously feel real pain or discomfort when you are trying to break a bad habit and actively start breaking it. So, pick something even MORE uncomfortable and make yourself do that thing whenever you refuse to give up your harmful habit or whenever you temporarily give it up and then foolishly fall back to it again.

Once more, let us suppose you know that smoking cigarettes will definitely harm you but you self-defeatingly keep smoking. Or suppose you keep unhealthfully gaining weight and had better stay with no more than 1,500 calories a day; then, instead, you keep getting up to 1,800, 2,000, or even 2,400 calories a day. How do you penalize yourself every time you go over your own set limits of smoking no cigarettes or eating only 1,500 calories? Quite simply. Set a strong and painful penalty—such as lighting every cigarette you smoke with a twenty dollar bill. Or talking to a boring and obnoxious acquaintance for at least an hour every time you take a single puff. Or running for two miles (if you hate running) whenever you eat more than 1,500 calories. Or eating a half pound of some food you find very distasteful or taking a sniff of an odor that you find utterly repulsive every single time you eat five calories more than 1,500.

Using the principles of immediate reinforcement and quick (and inevitable!) penalties on every occasion when you indulge in bad habits or refuse to engage in good habits (like exercising or doing at least an hour's work on a paper you are writing) won't absolutely make you give up your frustration intolerance and your tendency to foolishly indulge yourself in pernicious behavior. But it will definitely help!

17

REBT Insight No. 12: If You Backslide, Try, Try Again!

As noted in the previous chapter, human beings change for the better—then backslide. You, too!

If you use REBT to overcome your misery and you never fall back to it again—great. But never fear. You will sometimes fall back. Want to bet?

We prepare our clients at the Albert Ellis Institute by giving them the pamphlet, *How to Maintain and Enhance Your Rational Emotive Behavior Therapy Gains*. The second part of this pamphlet, "How to Deal with Backsliding," emphasizes REBT Insight No. 12: *When you improve your emotional disturbances, it will be a miracle if you never backslide. When you do, back to the REBT drawing board. Try, try again!*

The section of our pamphlet that deals with backsliding makes these points:

1. Accept your backsliding as normal—as something that happens to almost everyone who at first improves emotionally. See it as part of your being a fallible human. Don't damn yourself when some of your old problems return; and don't think that you have to handle them entirely by yourself and that it is wrong or weak for you to seek help from others.

2. When you backslide, look at your self-defeating *behavior* as bad and unfortunate, but work very hard at refusing to put *yourself* down for engaging in this behavior. Use the highly important REBT philosophy of refusing to rate *you*, your*self*, or your *being* but of measuring only your *acts*, *deeds*, and *traits*.

You are always a *person who* acts well or badly—and never a *good person* or a *bad person*. No matter how badly you fall back and make yourself upset again, you can always accept yourself *with* this poor behavior—and then keep trying to *change* this behavior.

3. Go back to the ABCs of REBT and see what you did to fall back to your old anxiety or depression. At A (Activating Event or Adversity), you probably experienced some failure or rejection once again. At rB (rational Belief) you probably told yourself that you didn't *like* failing and didn't *want* to be rejected. If you only stayed with these rational Beliefs, you would merely feel sorry, regretful, disappointed, or frustrated.

But when you felt depressed again, you probably then went on to irrational Beliefs (iBs), such as: "I *must* not fail! It's *horrible* when I do!" "I *have to* be accepted, because if I'm not that makes me an *unlovable, worthless person!*" Then, after convincing yourself of these iBs, you felt, at C (emotional Consequence), once again depressed and self-downing.

4. When you find irrational Beliefs with which you are once again disturbing yourself, just as you originally used Disputing (D) to surrender them, do so again—*immediately* and *persistently*. Thus, you can ask yourself, "Why *must* I not fail? Is it really *horrible* if I do?"

And you can answer: "There is *no* reason why I *must* not fail, though I can think of several reasons why it would be highly undesirable. It's not *horrible* if I do fail—only quite *inconvenient.*"

You can also Dispute your other irrational Beliefs by asking yourself, "Where is it written that I *have to* be accepted? How do I become an *unlovable, worthless person* if I am rejected?"

And you can answer: "I never *have to* be accepted, though I would very much *prefer* to be. If I am rejected, that makes me, alas, a *person who* is rejected this time. But it hardly makes me an *unlovable, worth-*

less person who will always be rejected by anyone for whom I really care."

5. Keep looking for and vigorously Disputing your irrational Beliefs. Keep doing this, over and over, until you build emotional muscle (just as you would build physical muscle by learning how to exercise and then *continuing* to exercise).

6. Don't fool yourself into believing that if you merely change your language you will always change your thinking. You may neurotically tell yourself, "I *must* succeed and be approved," and then you may sanely change this to, "I *prefer* to succeed and be approved." Underneath, however, you may still believe, "But I really *have to* do well and truly *must* be loved."

Before you stop your Disputing and before you are satisfied with your rational answers, keep on working until you are *really* convinced of these rational answers and until your anxiety, depression, and rage truly decline. Then do the same thing many, many times—until your new Effective Philosophy (E) becomes firm. It almost always will, if you keep reworking and repeating it.

If you convince yourself lightly (or "intellectually") of your new Effective Philosophy, it will tend to get through to you lightly—and briefly. Think it through *strongly* and *vigorously*, and do so many times.

Thus, you can *powerfully* convince yourself, until you really *feel* it: "I do not *need* what I *want*! I never *have to* succeed, no matter how greatly I *wish to* do so!" "I *can* stand being rejected by someone I care for. It won't *kill* me—and I *still* can lead a happy life!" "*No* person is damnable and worthless—including and especially *me*!"

Windy Dryden, one of the most creative practitioners of REBT, has invented a technique of dealing with your light rational Beliefs and turning them into strong, solid, truly emotional ones. Thus, if you lightly tell yourself, "I do not *need* what I *want*! I never *have to* succeed, no matter how strongly I *wish to* do so!" and you are not convinced that you feel the way you supposedly think, you can Dispute your rational Belief—yes, your rational Belief—to come up with answers that make it more convincing. For example:

Light rational belief: "I do not *need* what I want."

Disputing: "Why don't I need what I want?"

Answer: (a) "I can obviously live without getting what I want." (b) "Fate and the universe never *owe* me what I want." (c) "I can still be happy about many things if I don't get what I want." (d) "If I absolutely needed and achieved everything I wanted, I wouldn't have time to enjoy all my wants."

Light rational belief: "I never have to succeed, no matter how strongly I want to do so."

Disputing: "Why do I never have to succeed, no matter how strongly I want to do so?"

Answer: (a) "Obviously, I always *can* fail, no matter how hard I try to succeed." (b) "There is no law of the universe that says I *have to* succeed." (c) "I am a fallible human who will naturally and easily fail." (d) "All kinds of unfortunate conditions, like sickness and disability, can make me fail." (e) "Only if I were superhuman, which I am not, could I always succeed at everything."

If you strongly and persistently dispute your light rational Beliefs-feelings-actions, you will see that they are light and can turn them into stronger and more convincing Beliefs that you may actualize.

Tony, a member of my therapy group that included Georgiana (whose case I presented in the previous chapter), saw that Georgiana worked so well on overcoming her violent feelings of jealousy that he gave himself a similar homework assignment to help overcome his own backsliding. Tony was a forty-six-year-old owner of a retail store, severely anxious and depressed about his business. He desperately *needed*, especially at Christmas time, to do better than last year's sales. When he didn't, he was depressed for the next several months.

Tony was in one of my therapy groups for a year, and every few months we helped him to accept uncertainty and to stop worrying about his sales. Then he would fall back to renewed feelings of panic. Seeing Georgiana finally maintain her progress, he assigned himself to using the same techniques she used. He concentrated on these points:

1. He at first put himself down greatly for making himself panicked again about his store. But he worked at seeing that his backsliding only showed that he was a normal—though *not* a healthy—fallible human. He shamelessly talked about his renewed anxiety in group and acknowledged it to his family and friends.

2. He was able to see *it*, his backsliding, as bad but not view *himself* as a weak person for letting himself backslide. This *self*-acceptance enabled him to go back to working at getting over *it*.

3. Tony saw, once again, that, when his panic returned, he mainly held the irrational Belief (iB), "I *must* have good sales this year! It would be *horrible* if they fell off. I *couldn't bear* the hardships that would ensue!"

4. He forcefully and persistently asked himself, "Where is it written that I *must* have better sales this year?" Answer: "Only in my nutty head! I don't *have to*, though that would be lovely."

And: "In what way would it be *horrible* if sales fell off?" Answer: "In no way! It would only be damned frustrating. But not the end of my life!"

And: "Could I *really* not bear the hardships of a poor sales year?" Answer: "Obviously I could! I won't go out of business. My family won't starve. And I can work to make things better next year."

5. Tony kept actively and vigorously Disputing his irrational Beliefs until he found it easy to do so and until he regularly arrived at E, his Effective New Philosophies.

6. When he answered himself, at E, "Too bad. If I do poorly at sales, so I do poorly!" he stopped to inquire: "Do I *really* accept that 'too bad' or do I still really think 'It's awful'?" He answered: "Yes, dammit, whether I accept it or not, it *is* too bad. *Not* awful! *Not* unbearable! Just *too damned bad!*"

7. He strongly told himself, many times, "I never *need* good sales. I *can* live and be happy if I don't do better than last year. Loss of income is *never* a holy horror!"

By often working at these assignments, Tony reached a point where he only occasionally fell back to a state of panic. Fortunately—if we may call it that—he did have one of the worst Christmas seasons he ever had at his store. And although he was disappointed and sorry, he was rarely anxious and never depressed about it. As he reported to his therapy group:

"I lost a hell of a lot of sales and money this Christmas. But I gained a hell of a lot of *me*—of control over my anxiety. That's worth much more than money." The group agreed.

Tony went on to work on other problems—especially his decreased sex drive. His poor retail business, for the first time in years, was easy to accept.

Following the above REBT plan, you can stop your own backsliding and can regain any progress that you have made and temporarily lost—if you keep working to do so!

REBT Exercise No. 17

Use rational emotive imagery (REI) to get over any emotional upsetness that you may have about falling back to a previous level of disturbance; or use it for almost any other problem of anxiety, depression, or rage that you may have.

In using rational emotive imagery, you first imagine one of the worst things that might happen to you: for example, you worked very hard to overcome your fear of public speaking or to overcome your addiction to cigarettes, and now you have fallen back again, and in fact have a worse fear than you ever had or are smoking even more cigarettes a day than you ever did before in your life.

You let yourself feel anxious, depressed, or self-hating about how you have just fallen back after previously working hard and effectively using REBT to overcome your fear or your addiction. Let us suppose that as you vividly imagine this worst possible thing happening, you feel exceptionally ashamed, guilty, and self-downing about your allowing yourself to fall back. Get fully in touch, now, with your disturbed feeling and let yourself fully—yes, fully!—experience it for a brief time. Don't avoid your feeling of guilt or self-downing. On the contrary, face it and make yourself truly *feel it*.

When you have actually felt, really felt, this disturbed emotion for a while, push yourself—yes, *push* yourself—to change this feeling in your gut, so that instead you *only* experience a healthy (but still strong) feeling. Thus, make yourself feel keenly disappointed, regretful, annoyed, or irritated with your behavior (for you *have* done a wrong self-defeating thing by letting yourself fall back to your original fear or addiction), but get rid of, actually change, your unhealthy feeling of shame, guilt, depression, or self-downing.

As I point out in a pamphlet on rational emotive imagery (REI) that is published by the Albert Ellis Institute (and that is included in the final chapter of *A Guide to Rational Living*), don't think that you can't do this, can't change your feeling—for you invariably can. Don't forget that *you*—not the Man in the Moon!—created your upsetness in the first place; so *you*—yes, *you*—can always change it in the second place. You can, at almost any time you work at doing so, get in touch with your gut-level feelings and push yourself to change them so that you experience different feelings. You definitely have the ability to do this. So try, concentrate—and do it!

When you have let yourself push yourself *only* to feel sorry, regretful, disappointed, or irritated (instead of ashamed, guilty, depressed, and self-downing), look at what you have done in your head to *make yourself* have these new, healthy (though still negative) feelings. You will see, if you observe yourself clearly, that you have in some manner changed your Belief System (or irrational Beliefs or Bullshit) at B, and have thereby changed your emotional Consequences at C, so that you now feel healthy instead of unhealthy emotions. Become fully aware of the rational Beliefs (rBs) that you have used to create your new healthy emotional Consequences (Cs) regarding the unpleasant Activating Experiences (A) that you have imagined or fantasized.

Thus, in this particular case, A was the observation that you have fallen back to your old phobia or addiction. At iB, you told yourself something like, "I should not have fallen back! How awful and shameful to fall back! I'm a pretty incompetent person to let myself do a foolish thing like that!" Then you felt depressed, guilty, self-hating. Now, if you do the rational emotive imagery correctly, you have changed to a new set of rBs (rational Beliefs), such as: "It was most unfortunate and unpleasant that I fell back but that is the nature of humans, including myself, to take two steps forward and one step backward. And sometimes two or three steps backward! I'm hardly an incompetent person to let myself do a foolish thing like that, but a fairly competent person who sometimes acts incompetently. And that is my nature, too!—to at times act foolishly. What a pain in the butt! But I can do better than that, I am sure, in the future, and get right back to the progress that I formerly made. Okay: back to the drawing board!"

Observe and understand that these new, rational Beliefs are the ones that made you change your feelings. So, practice changing your disturbed feelings again and again, by repeating the rational Beliefs. If your upsetting feelings do not change as you attempt to feel more healthily, keep fantasizing the same unpleasant experiences or events and keep working on your gut and your head until you *do* change your feelings to healthy ones. Never forget: *You* create and control your feelings. Therefore, *you* can invariably change them.

Once you succeed in feeling sorry, regretful, disappointed, irritated, and frustrated rather than anxious, depressed, guilty, and self-downing about your falling back (or about any of your other disruptive emotions and behaviors), and once you see exactly what Beliefs you have changed in your head to make yourself feel badly but not emotionally upset, keep repeating this process. Make yourself feel really disturbed. Then, make yourself feel displeased but not disturbed. Now, see exactly what you did in your head to change your feelings and practice doing this same kind of thing, over and over again. Keep practicing, until you can easily, after you imagine highly unfortunate experiences (such as falling back in your self-therapy after you have previously made some progress) at point A, feel upset at point C, change your feelings at point C to those of disappointment and sorrow but not upsetness, and see what you keep doing at point B to change your Belief system that creates and maintains your feelings. If you keep practicing this kind of rational emotive imagery (REI) at least once (and preferably two or three times) every day for the next few weeks, you will tend to reach the point where whenever you think of this same kind of unpleasant event, or it actually occurs in your life, you will unconsciously and automatically feel displeased and sorry rather than unhealthily depressed and self-downing.

REI, then, can be done imaginatively before an unfortunate event (like falling back in your progress) occurs. It can also be done at the same time that the event actually occurs. And if you miss doing it when it occurs, it can be done an hour later, or a day or two later. In all cases, you let yourself feel guilty, ashamed, depressed, or anxious, and then you push yourself to feel disappointed and frustrated but *not* truly upset.

Suppose you promise yourself to do REI at least once a day about your falling back from your REBT progress (or about anything else that you upset yourself about) and suppose that you keep postponing it and failing to do it. You can then use reinforcement by rewarding yourself with something you really like to do (such as reading, eating, television viewing, or social contacts with your friends) *after* you have done the rational imagery as often as you have promised yourself to do it. Moreover, you can penalize yourself with something you really dislike (such as eating something obnoxious, contributing to a cause you hate, burning a twenty-dollar bill, or getting up a half hour earlier in the morning) when you have *not* done REI as you have promised yourself to do it. You may do REI without this kind of reinforcement or penalizing, but if you have trouble doing it this way, then you may help yourself by resorting to reinforcement methods. Similarly, if you procrastinate on any other important task, you can reward yourself *after* you do it and penalize yourself when you don't. This system won't absolutely *make* you do what you want to do. But it will often help!

18

REBT Insight No. 13: You Can Extend Your Refusal to Make Yourself Miserable

REBT gives you two kinds of solutions to your emotional problems: (a) Immediate, limited, and short-lived answers and (b) Long-lived, extended, and elegant answers. Even its less elegant and short-range answers are pretty good, for they show you how to quickly rid yourself of feelings of anxiety, depression, self-hatred, hostility, and self-pity. And how to reduce your lethargy, incompetence, procrastination, phobias, compulsions, and addictions.

But REBT's extended and long-lasting solutions are better. For they show you:

How to maintain your improvement

How to rarely upset yourself again in the same way

How to quickly recover when you fall back

How to generalize from your original disturbance to other upsets that you may experience

How to overcome—and maintain your victory over—any kind of neurotic problem for the rest of your life

How to stubbornly refuse to make yourself miserable over anything—yes, anything

For REBT says that your neurotic problems stem from three basic kinds of godlike, *must*urbatory thinking and that if you surrender your unrealistic and unscientific dogmas, you can see that all your emotional problems stem from similar irrational Beliefs. You can then extend your REBT answers to your other destructive behaviors. REBT thereby gives you specific *and* general solutions to emotional pain.

This brings us to Insight No. 13: *Once you understand the basic irrational Beliefs (iBs) you create to upset yourself, you can use this understanding to explore, attack, and surrender your other present and future emotional problems.*

How do you broaden your use of REBT from solving one set of emotional problems to reducing your other miseries? Here are some ways to extend your results to other possible troubles:

1. Show yourself that your present upsetness and the ways in which you create it are not unique. Admit that virtually all your emotional problems are partly created by your own irrational Beliefs (iBs). Therefore—fortunately!—you can *un*create these iBs by firmly and steadily disputing and acting against them.

2. Once again, recognize that you mainly use these irrational Beliefs (iBs) to disturb yourself:

   a. "I *must* do well and *have to* be approved by people whom I find important." This iB makes you feel anxious, depressed, and self-hating, and it leads you to avoid doing things at which you may fail and to run away from relationships that may not turn out well.

   b. "Other people *must* treat me fairly and nicely!" This iB makes you feel angry, furious, violent, and over-rebellious.

   c. "The conditions under which I live *must* be comfortable and free from major hassles!" This iB creates feelings of frustration intolerance and self-pity and sometimes those of anger and depression. It also leads to procrastination, compulsions, and addictions.

3. Recognize that when you employ these three dogmatic *musts*

you easily derive several other irrational conclusions from them. Such as:

a. "Because I am not doing as well as I *must*, I am an incompetent, worthless person!" (self-downing)

b. "Since I am not being approved by important people, as I *have to be*, it's *awful* and *terrible*! It's the end of the world!" (awfulizing; terribleizing; catastrophizing)

c. "Because others are not treating me as fairly and as nicely as they *absolutely should* treat me, they are *utterly rotten people* and deserve to be damned!" (damnation)

d. "Since the conditions under which I live are not as comfortable as they *should be*, and since my life has several major hassles, as it *must* not have, I *can't stand* it! My existence is a horror!" (can't-stand-it-itis)

e. "Because I have failed as I *ought* not and have been rejected as I *absolutely should not* have been, I'll *always* fail and *never* get accepted as I *must* be! My life will be hopeless and joyless forever!" (overgeneralizing; hopelessness)

4. Work at seeing that these irrational Beliefs *often* and *generally* upset you. See that you bring them to *many* different kinds of undesirable situations.

   Realize that in just about all cases where you feel anxious and depressed and where you act foolishly, you are consciously or unconsciously sneaking in one or more of these iBs. Consequently, if you reject them in one and are still disturbed about something else, you can use the same REBT principles to discover your irrational Beliefs in the new area and to eliminate them there.

5. Keep showing yourself that it is almost impossible to disturb yourself in *any* way if you abandon your rigid, dogmatic *shoulds*, *oughts*, and *musts* and if you replace them with flexible (though still strong) *desires* and *preferences*.

6. Continue to acknowledge that you can change your irrational Beliefs (iBs) by powerfully using the scientific method. With scientific thinking, including reflection on your emotions and behaviors, you can show yourself that your irra-

tional Beliefs are only assumptions—not facts. You can logically and realistically Dispute them in many ways, such as these:

a. You can show yourself that your iBs are self-defeating—that they interfere with your goals and your happiness. For if you rigidly convince yourself, "I *must* succeed at important tasks and *have to* be approved by all the important people I meet," you will at times fail and be disapproved—and thereby make yourself feel anxious and depressed instead of sorry and frustrated.

b. Your irrational Beliefs do not conform to reality—and especially do not conform to the fact that humans are imperfect and fallible.

   If you always *had* to succeed, if the universe commanded that you *must* do so, you obviously *would* always succeed. And of course you often don't!

   If you invariably *had* to be approved by others, you could never be disappointed. But clearly you frequently are!

   The universe plainly does *not* always give you everything you demand. So although your desires are often realistic, your godlike commands definitely are not!

c. Your irrational Beliefs do not follow from your rational premises or assumptions and are therefore illogical and absurd. "I strongly *want* to succeed" doesn't lead to "Therefore I *must*!" No matter how desirable justice is, it never, therefore, *has to* exist.

   Although the scientific method is not infallible or sacred, it helps you discover which of your beliefs are irrational and self-defeating and how to use facts and logical thinking to give them up. If you think scientifically, you will avoid dogma and keep your hypotheses about yourself, about other people, and about the world always open to change.

7. Try to establish some main goals and purposes in life—goals

that you would *like* very much to reach but that you never *absolutely must* attain. Keep checking to see how you are coming along with these goals. At times revise them. See how you feel when you achieve them. You don't *have to* have long-range goals. But they help!

8. If you get bogged down and begin to lead a life that seems miserable or dull, review the points made here and work at using them. There's rarely any gain without pain!

Many of my clients, alas, refuse to extend their use of REBT, even though it helped them to quickly—sometimes "miraculously"—overcome the problems that drove them to therapy. Because, often, they have low frustration tolerance (FI) and refuse to march on to extended and elegant REBT solutions.

Not so Malvina. When she first came to REBT, she was a highly attractive nineteen-year-old student, majoring in history. Although bright and talented (especially in music), she was a social basket case. She was too shy to date. She had no close female friends. She considered herself plain and not too intelligent. She was severely depressed and often thought about suicide. She had no real career goals. She hated her parents—both of whom were severely depressed, too—and blamed them for her troubles.

Three years of psychoanalysis had done little for Malvina but only helped her become more hostile toward her family and dependent on her analyst. Although her friends did their best to get her away from the analyst, nothing worked until he had a heart attack, retired, and moved to Florida. She tried to keep in touch with him by phone, but he finally refused her calls. The only reason she agreed to see me was that at that time I was his exact age, fifty-one, and looked somewhat like him.

For many months I got nowhere with Malvina, as I tried to show her that her own crooked, self-damning thoughts—and not the "horrible teachings" of her parents—mainly created her feelings of depression. At first, she wouldn't accept these REBT hypotheses.

I continued showing her that she had several strong irrational Beliefs—especially, "I *must* always be exceptionally beautiful, bright, and lovable and I'm worthless when I fall short of this!" She finally admitted, "I guess you're right. I am idiotically depressing myself." But instead of working to give this up, she immediately started berating herself "for being so stupidly irrational," and she became, if possible, more depressed.

On several occasions, Malvina talked so much about suicide that I encouraged her to go for antidepressants and to consider entering a hospital. She refused to consider medication, but the threat of being hospitalized encouraged her to work at accepting and using REBT.

First, Malvina stopped blaming herself for being so disturbed. She worked hard to stop upsetting herself *about* being upset, and she began to accept herself *with* her depression.

Although when Malvina stopped damning herself for being disturbed she became one of the most *relaxed* depressives I have ever seen, she still often blamed herself for her "plainness" (she had "too large" a nose), for her "stupidity" (she only received Bs instead of As at math), and for her lack of career goals. But—because she now really saw the ABCs of REBT and saw how Disputing helped her give up the irrational Belief that she *must* not be depressed—she decided to work at overcoming *all* her self-damning.

She did. Malvina first accepted herself with her "plainness"—and then saw that she was fairly attractive. She stopped blaming herself for her "stupidity"—and then realized she was intelligent. She convinced herself that it was *too bad* but not *awful* that she had no career vocational goals—and then started planning to get some.

Although she now realized she was attractive and bright, Malvina used rational emotive imagery to vividly imagine herself becoming *really* ugly and stupid. She then made herself feel only sorry and regretful, instead of depressed, because she told herself that even under these grim conditions, she still could—and *would*—accept herself and strive to lead a fairly happy existence.

After several months of refusing to belittle herself, Malvina for the first time in her life felt undepressed. Better yet, she realized that she could soon reduce her other feelings of anxiety and shame by strongly counterattacking all her self-put-downs.

To make her gains more solid, Malvina also tackled her awfulizing and concluded, "It's not *awful*—only *annoying*—that I am not very good in math!" She worked against her can't-stand-it-itis until she convinced herself, "I *can* bear my large nose though I'll never like it." Furthermore, she fought stoutly against her ideas of hopelessness and replaced them with, "Although I haven't come up with a suitable career yet, there's no reason why I *never* will. It's hard to find something I really will like. But it's hardly hopeless!"

In addition to using scientific thinking and firmly attacking her dogmatic *musts*, Malvina began helping her friends see and Dispute their own irrational Beliefs. She did so well in this respect that she finally found her career. She went for graduate work in clinical psychology and for the past fifteen years has been an excellent rational emotive behavior therapist. She enjoys her work immensely. She has several close friends. After a few years of comfortable dating, she successfully married and is the happy (and rational!) mother of a nine-year-old daughter.

Is Malvina now happy *because* she is a successful psychologist, wife, mother, and friend? Yes. But she insists, when I see her at professional meetings, that she would be undepressed and unanxious even if she had failed in these respects. I believe her because she has worked exceptionally hard at extending the ABCs and DEs of REBT to *any* feelings of anxiety and depression she may experience. So she has achieved the elegant rational emotive behavior therapy solution.

You, once you use REBT to overcome any of your main problems, may not have to work as hard as Malvina to generalize and extend it to your other emotional difficulties. But if you do, you do! If you follow REBT's Insight No. 13, you can use the rational ideas that helped you overcome one problem to show yourself how you can conquer other neurotic difficulties. Once again—if you *work* at doing so!

REBT Exercise No. 18

Imagine that you have overcome one of your greatest anxieties—such as your fear of writing, public speaking, sexual rejections, or doing poorly at work. You are feeling fine about this, but now you see that you have developed a new fear—say, talking to people at parties or other social gatherings.

First, see if you feel really upset—downed or depressed—about this new anxiety. If you do, use rational emotive imagery to make yourself feel *only* disappointed with your behavior, but not horrified about you, the person who has fallen back. To change your unhealthy feeling, tell yourself rational self-statements, such as: "I don't like my foolishly falling back and creating a new irrational fear, but that doesn't make me a *total* fool!" Or: "Too bad I created another silly anxiety, but I'm still fallible in that respect and I can work at becoming somewhat less fallible but never perfect."

Once you really begin to accept *you* in spite of your new irrational *behavior*, look for the things in common between the irrational Beliefs (iBs) creating your new anxiety and those that you worked on to give up your old anxiety. For example, suppose you previously feared doing poorly at work and you now fear socializing at parties.

Your previous iB may have been: "I must impress my fellow workers." Your new iB may be: "I must impress the people I meet at social gatherings."

Again, your old iB may have been: "My fellow workers must not put me down. If they do and I don't tell them off, I'm a real schnook!" Your new iB may be: "People at social gatherings must not scorn me and laugh at me. If they do and I don't very wittily get back at them, I'm a schnook and an idiot!"

When you discover the common irrational Beliefs that led to the original anxiety you overcame and you see how they are repeated to create your new set of anxieties, use the same kind of Disputing and the same kind of other REBT techniques that you successfully used to overcome your previous irrational fears and persist at them until you also can use them to overcome your new fears.

Since there are only a few basic iBs that lead to anxiety, depression, guilt, hostility, and self-downing, when you see that you have a new disturbed feeling, or a variation of one of the old ones, assume that you *once again* can find the iBs that you are using to create your new symptoms. And when you do find these iBs—which you will, if you *persist*—use techniques of Disputing and other REBT procedures that you found worked well on the old emotional problems. Don't give up! Keep working at it! And almost invariably you will find that similar neurotic symptoms stem from similar iBs. Try generalizing in this respect—and see how well it often works!

The same thing goes for your self-defeating behaviors. You may have been compulsively addicted, say, to overeating and you overcame your addiction by discovering your iBs—such as, "I *need* this delicious food, I *can't stand* being deprived of it!"—and by changing them. Now you may be compulsively addicted to smoking or to caffeine, and you can often find similar *needs* and *I-can't-stand-its* that are making you addicted. If you formerly proved to yourself that you *don't* need delicious food and *can* stand being deprived of it, you can similarly now prove to yourself that you do *not* need smoking or caffeine and definitely *can* stand their loss. Just as you once forced yourself to *uncomfortably* push away the extra food, you can now force yourself to push away the unnecessary cigarettes and coffee. You were uncomfortable but did not die the first time. Nor will you die of discomfort now!

You can also generalize from your successful use of emotive REBT techniques. Thus, you may have overcome your guilt about not visiting your in-laws every week by very vigorously telling yourself, "I'm not upsetting them by refusing to see them as often as they demand. *They* are responsible for their own upsetness. Too bad! If they hate me, they hate me! I can live *with* that. At worst, I'm rotten to my in-laws, but that doesn't make me a *rotten person!*" To get over guilt or shame about other things—such as disclosing one of your weaknesses to people or not being the greatest parent who ever lived—you can generalize from your past REBT success and use a similar emotive method to overcome the new aspect of your self-downing.

Whenever, then, you have used REBT to reduce one aspect of your disturbance, ask yourself how you can use it to overcome other aspects. And *practice* using this REBT technique again and again in somewhat similar circumstances until it becomes second nature for you to employ it in various areas of your disturbance.

19

REBT Insight No. 14: Yes, You *Can* Stubbornly Refuse to Make Yourself Severely Anxious or Depressed About *Anything*

Suppose the very worst—yes, the *worst*—happens, can you still stubbornly refuse to make yourself severely anxious or depressed about anything?

Yes. Definitely, yes.

Don't forget that you are a *creative* human being. If you even *partly* use your creativity, you can be unmiserable—and at times even happy—under some of the most unfortunate conditions.

Let me illustrate with an extreme case, which was told to me years ago by a famous American musician. He knew an elderly retired couple who had lost their only child, a bright and very attractive boy, when he died of pneumonia at the age of six. They took this loss very well, and continued to do so even after they tried unsuccessfully to have another child.

For many years after their son's death, people would say to them, "Isn't it sad that you lost such a charming child? Imagine how nice it would be if he were still alive. He would be such a comfort to you. He'd probably be married by now and you'd have grandchildren to lighten your life as you grow older. Of course, you are very sad about such a great loss!"

"Oh no," this couple would immediately respond. "We don't feel sad at all when we think about Marvie and his death."

"You don't?" would come the astonished query.

"No, of course not. He was such a fine boy and led such a good life while he was here. And now that he's gone, we are sure that God is taking the best care of him in heaven, and that he is, and will always be, very happy there. So we are not at all sad about what happened to him."

Both these parents would then genuinely beam and convince everyone, especially themselves, how happy they were in the face of this grim loss.

Cover-up? Defensive denial? I would say, yes. Did this couple repress their underlying feelings of sadness, perhaps even depression? Again, probably yes. So I by no means recommend their refusing to acknowledge their severe loss. In fact, I am highly suspicious of it.

The main point I am making, however, is this: People *can* change their feelings. No matter what happens to them, they *can* creatively decide to feel one way or another about it. And they have quite a range of possible feelings to choose from!

Do you really want to test out this freedom of choice in your own life? All right, let's experiment. Let us imagine some of the worst things that might happen to you—things that you would clearly dislike and about which you might easily make yourself anxious, depressed, or enraged. I am going to present some of these grim events to you and ask you, if you strongly use the REBT insights we have been discussing in this book, how you would rationally cope with them and make yourself feel appropriately sad, displeased, and annoyed but *not* unhealthily panicked and destroyed.

Ready?

Question: Suppose you find, after a long search, a job that is ideal for you and suppose you foolishly come late for work, are lazy, act nastily to your boss, and get fired. What can you rationally and emotionally tell yourself?

REBT answer: You can tell yourself: "Too bad! I certainly behaved poorly this time. But that hardly makes me a stupid or incompetent person. Just someone who needlessly did myself in. Now what can I do to find another job like this one, work hard at it, and please my boss? But even if I never get as good a job again, I am determined to do the best I can and to be as effective and as happy as I can be with a worse position."

Question: Suppose you have a serious accident and lose an arm or a leg—or even your vision—how can you manage to live with those kinds of handicaps?

REBT answer: Not so well! You certainly would feel greatly deprived and frustrated. But not necessarily depressed! If you tell yourself, "Although my abilities and pleasures are seriously limited, I can still do many interesting and enjoyable things and can find ways to compensate for my disabilities. Instead of focusing dismally on what I can *not* do, I can concentrate on the many interests and pleasures I can *still* have and thereby almost guarantee myself a reasonably happy existence."

Question: Suppose you bought a stock at a low price, felt anxious about how high it might go, and sold it only at a small profit, instead of the large amount you could have made if you had held on to it a while longer. Can you still refuse to make yourself miserable about that?

REBT answer: You damned well can! Even if you stupidly sold at exactly the wrong time and lost money on the stock, while everybody else held on until they made a mint, you could make yourself feel disappointed—but not self-hating—about your loss. You could convince yourself, "If I choose to gamble at anything, I had better acknowledge that it *is* a gamble and that there is never a certainty of winning. Second, no one buys and sells stocks and always makes maximum gains. Including me! Third, it was good that I made *anything* on the deal. What luck! Fourth, this gives me a chance to see what I am doing to foolishly make myself anxious about this deal, and what I can do in the future to make myself less anxious. Fifth, making a pile of money is good and will make me happier. But I can also be distinctly happy with less money. *If* I stop berating myself for making less!"

Question: Suppose your beloved mate or one of your close friends for whom you really care dies. How can you rationally deal with that great loss?

REBT answer: By steadfastly *accepting*, without at all *liking*, what you can't change. Firmly tell yourself, "Death, so far, is inevitable for all of us. Nor could I have prevented this death. I shall miss this person considerably and feel truly deprived of companionship and pleasure. But I can still think of the fine times we did have. And I can realize that he or she gave me great joy, but the feeling I had was *my* feeling and I *can* have similar feelings and pleasure with others. What can I *now* do to increase my ability to love and to find suitable partners to care for?"

Question: Suppose you no longer can enjoy the main things you used to enjoy—such as sports, work, romantic love, or sex. Isn't that good reason to feel depressed?

REBT answer: Definitely not! You would then clearly have *less* satisfaction, *less* pleasure in life. But hardly *none*. Unless you foolishly depress yourself by telling yourself, "I *must* still have these former enjoyments." Then you *will* ruin your life and enjoy virtually *nothing*. But if you no longer can thrill at sports, work, sex, or anything else, you can almost certainly, as long as you are truly alive, find *something* that you really like. What? Seek, experiment, and find out. Just thinking can be enjoyable. Or even television! As long as you stop convincing yourself that life without *certain* pleasure is *totally* unsatisfying!

Question: Suppose you are in constant physical pain (for example, from advanced cancer), you really don't enjoy anything, and you are pretty certain that this painful existence will continue until you die. What can you then do to avoid real misery?

REBT answer: Very little, physically. And emotionally you would hardly be happy! If I were in that sad condition and had no important goal to keep fulfilling—such as to help my loved ones or to finish a major project—I might rationally, calmly, decide to painlessly kill myself. For though I definitely find life good, it is hardly sacred, and it is not good under *all* conditions. So if my pain blocked all satisfactions, I would see little sense in living. But I wouldn't desperately depart. I would feel thankful for the life I had had, feel sorry that it was now so painful, and feel glad that I could think of some quick way of ending it. My other choice might well be to focus on some important thing I could do—such as finish a major book I was writing—and bear my pain until I at least finished this project. In either case, I would use rational thinking to show myself that even the "worst" conditions are not "horrible."

Question: Suppose you find a most unusual love partner with whom you are very happy and you then act so meanly with this person that he or she leaves you and goes off with someone else. How can you stubbornly refuse to make yourself depressed?

REBT answer: By doing exactly that: stubbornly refusing to make yourself depressed. You can tell yourself, "That was mean *behavior*—but that never makes me a mean and rotten *person*! I'd better admit that I made myself unlovable this time and ruined a fine relationship. But again, this foolish *conduct* doesn't by any means make me a totally unlovable *individual*. If I recognize my great loss and truly regret it, I can work hard at being less mean and more caring in the future and do my best to win back my partner's love. Or if that is impossible, I can push myself to look for another mate, act much better next time, and work to establish a fine relationship."

Question: Suppose that you know for sure that you're soon to die in an atomic holocaust and that, in fact, the whole human race will perish with you and completely die out. How would you feel, and what would you do?

REBT answer: Let me, once again, give my own answer. For a few minutes, I would make myself feel damned sad and frustrated. "What fools these mortals be! How foolish and unnecessary!" I would tell myself. "But if that's the way humans are, that's the way they are! Tough!" Then I would try my best to have a damned good time—eating, loving, and having sex while listening to great music!—during the last minutes or days of my one and only earthly existence.

What do all these questions and answers show? That much of your discomfort, pain, failure, rejection, and loss cannot be avoided or eliminated. Life, as we say in REBT, is frequently spelled H-A-S-S-L-E. A good deal of it, with thought and effort, you can greatly improve. Not all! Not completely!

Tough. But not awful, not horrible, not terrible. Just tough.

Now—how are you going to arrange for greater *enjoyment*?

Appendix 1: The Biological Basis of Human Irrationality

Before stating any hypothesis about the basis of human irrationality, definitions of the main terms employed in this appendix, *biological basis* and *irrationality*, are presented. *Biological basis* means that a characteristic or trait has distinctly innate (as well as distinctly acquired) origins—that it partly arises from the organism's natural, easy predisposition to behave in certain stipulated ways. This does not mean that this characteristic or trait has a purely instinctive basis, that it cannot undergo major change; nor does it mean that the organism would perish, or at least live in abject misery, without it. It simply means that, because of its genetic and/or congenital nature, an individual easily develops this trait and has a difficult time modifying or eliminating it.

Irrationality means any thought, emotion, or behavior that leads to self-defeating or self-destructive consequences—that significantly interferes with the survival and happiness of the organism. More specifically, irrational behavior usually has several aspects:

1. The individual believes, often devoutly, that it accords with the tenets of reality although in some important respect it really does not.
2. People who adhere to irrational behavior significantly denigrate or refuse to accept themselves.
3. Irrational behavior interferes with their getting along satisfactorily with members of their primary social groups.
4. Irrational behavior seriously blocks their achieving the kind of interpersonal relations that they would like to achieve.
5. Irrational behavior hinders their working gainfully and joyfully at some kind of productive labor.

6. Irrational behavior interferes with their own best interests in other important respects.

The major hypothesis of this appendix is as follows: Humans ubiquitously and constantly act irrationally in many important respects. Just about all of them do so during all their lives, though some considerably more than others. There is, therefore, some reason to believe that they do so naturally and easily, often against the teachings of their families and their culture, frequently against their own conscious wish and determination. Although modifiable to a considerable extent, their irrational tendencies seem largely ineradicable and intrinsically go with their biological (as well as sociological) nature.

This hypothesis goes back to the statements of some of the earliest historians and philosophers and has received adequate documentation over the years by a host of authorities, such as J. G. Frazier, Claude Levi-Strauss, Eric Hoffer, Walter B. Pitkin, and O. Rachleff. R. S. Parker noted that "most people are self-destructive, they behave in ways that are obviously against their best interest." Nonetheless, whenever I address an audience of psychologists or psychotherapists and point out this fairly obvious conclusion and state or imply that it arises out of the biological tendency of humans to behave irrationally, a great many dyed-in-the-wool environmentalists almost always rise with horror, foam at the mouth, and call me a traitor to objective, scientific thinking.

Hence this appendix. Following is a brief summary—for the amount of supporting evidence assumes overwhelming proportions and would literally take many volumes to summarize properly—of some of the main reasons behind the thesis that human irrationality roots itself in basic human nature. The summary is confined to outlining the multiplicity of major irrationalities and to giving some of the logical and psychological reasons why it seems almost certain that they have biological origins.

First are listed some of the outstanding irrationalities among the thousands collected over the years. The following manifestations of human behavior certainly do not appear completely irrational—for they also have (as what behavior has not?) some distinct advantages. Some people, such as those Eric Hoffer calls true believers, will even hold that many of them bring about much more good than harm. Almost any reasonably objective observer of human affairs, however, will probably tend to agree that they include a large amount of foolishness, unreality, and danger to our survival or happiness.

1. Custom and Conformity Irrationalities
    a. Outdated and rigid customs
    b. Ever-changing, expensive fashions
    c. Fads and popular crazes
    d. Customs involving royalty and nobility
    e. Customs involving holidays and festivals
    f. Customary gifts and presentations
    g. Customs in connection with social affairs and dating
    h. Courtship, marriage, and wedding customs
    i. Puberty rites, bar mitzvahs, etc.
    j. Academic rites and rituals
    k. Hazings of schools, fraternal organizations, etc.
    l. Religious rites and rituals
    m. Customs and rites regarding scientific papers
    n. Circumcision conventions and rituals
    o. Rigid rules of etiquette and manners
    p. Blue laws
    q. Strong disposition to obey authority, even when it makes unreasonable demands
2. Ego-Related Irrationalities
    a. Tendency to deify oneself
    b. Dire need to have superiority over others
    c. Tendency to give oneself a global, total, all-inclusive rating
    d. Tendency to desperately seek for status
    e. Tendency to prove oneself rather than enjoy oneself

    f. Tendency to believe that one's value as a human depends on one's competency at an important performance or a group of important performances

    g. Tendency to value oneself or devalue oneself in regard to the performances of one's family

    h. Tendency to value or devalue oneself in regard to the performances or status of one's school, neighborhood group, community, state, or country.

    i. Tendency to denigrate or devil-ify oneself.

3. Prejudice-Related Irrationalities

    a. Strong prejudice

    b. Dogma

    c. Racial prejudice

    d. Sex prejudice

    e. Political prejudice

    f. Social and class prejudice

    g. Religious prejudice

    h. Appearance prejudice

4. Common Kinds of Illogical Thinking

    a. Overgeneralization

    b. Magnification and exaggeration

    c. Use of non sequiturs

    d. Strong belief in anti-empirical statements

    e. Strong belief in absolutes

    f. Gullibility and over-suggestibility

    g. Strong belief in contradictory statements

    h. Strong belief in utopianism

    i. Strong adherence to unreality

    j. Strong belief in unprovable statements

    k. Shortsightedness

    l. Overcautiousness

    m. Giving up one extreme statement and going to the other extreme

    n. Strong belief in shoulds, oughts, and musts

    o. The dire need for certainty

    p. Wishful thinking

  q. Lack of self-perspective

  r. Difficulty of learning

  s. Difficulty of unlearning and relearning

  t. Deep conviction that because one believes something strongly it must have objective reality and truth

  u. Conviction that because one had better respect the rights of others to hold beliefs different from one's own, their beliefs have truth

5. Experiential and Feeling Irrationalities

  a. Strong conviction that because one experiences something deeply and "feels" its truth, it must have objective reality and truth

  b. Strong conviction that the more intensely one experiences something the more objective reality and truth it has

  c. Strong conviction that because one authentically and honestly feels something it must have objective truth in reality

  d. Strong conviction that all authentic and deeply experienced feelings represent legitimate and healthy feelings

  e. Strong conviction that when a powerful thought or feeling exists (e.g., a mystical feeling that one understands everything in the universe), it constitutes a deeper, more important, and factually truer idea than a rational thought or feeling

6. Habit-Making Irrationalities

  a. The acquiring of nonproductive and self-defeating habits easily and unconsciously

  b. The automatic retention and persistence of nonproductive and self-defeating habits in spite of one's conscious awareness of their irrationality

  c. Failure to follow up on conscious determination and resolution to break a self-defeating habit

  d. Inventing rationalizations and excuses for not giving up a self-defeating habit

    e. Backsliding into self-defeating habits after one has temporarily overcome them

7. Addictions to Self-Defeating Behaviors
    a. Addiction to overeating
    b. Addiction to smoking
    c. Addiction to alcohol
    d. Addiction to drugs
    e. Addiction to tranquilizers and other medicines
    f. Addiction to work, at the expense of greater enjoyments
    g. Addiction to approval and love

8. Neurotic and Psychotic Symptoms
    a. Overweening and disruptive anxiety
    b. Depression and despair
    c. Hostility and rage
    d. Extreme feelings of self-downing and hurt
    e. Extreme feelings of self-pity
    f. Childish grandiosity
    g. Refusal to accept reality
    h. Paranoid thinking
    i. Delusions
    j. Hallucinations
    k. Psychopathy
    l. Mania
    m. Extreme withdrawal or catatonia

9. Religious Irrationalities
    a. Devout faith unfounded on fact
    b. Slavish adherence to religious dogma
    c. Deep conviction that a supernatural force must exist
    d. Deep conviction that a supernatural force or entity has special, personal interest in oneself
    e. Deep conviction in heaven and hell
    f. Religious bigotry
    g. Persecution of other religious groups
    h. Wars between religious groups
    i. Scrupulous adherence to religious rules, rites, and taboos
    j. Religious antisexuality and extreme Puritanism

    k. Religious conviction that all pleasure equates with sin
    l. Complete conviction that some deity will heed one's prayers
    m. Absolute conviction that one has a spirit or soul entirely divorced from one's material body
    n. Absolute conviction that one's soul will live forever
    o. Absolute conviction that no kind of superhuman force can possibly exist

10. Population Irrationalities
    a. Population explosion in many parts of the world
    b. Lack of education in contraceptive methods
    c. Families having more children than they can afford to support
    d. Restrictions on birth control and abortion for those who want to use them
    e. Some nations deliberately fomenting a population explosion

11. Health Irrationalities
    a. Air pollution
    b. Noise pollution
    c. Drug advertising and promotion
    d. Poor health education
    e. Harmful food additives
    f. Uncontrolled medical costs and resultant poor health facilities
    g. Unnecessary surgical procedures
    h. Avoidance of physicians and dentists by people requiring diagnostic and medical procedures
    i. Neglect of medical research

12. Acceptance of Unreality
    a. Widespread acceptance and following of silly myths
    b. Widespread acceptance and following of extreme romanticism
    c. Widespread acceptance and following of foolish, inhumane fairy tales
    d. Widespread acceptance and following of unrealistic movies

e. Widespread acceptance and following of unrealistic radio and TV dramas and serials
f. Widespread Pollyannaism
g. Widespread utopianism

13. Political Irrationalities
    a. Wars
    b. Undeclared wars and cold wars
    c. Civil wars
    d. Political corruption and graft
    e. Foolish election and voting procedures
    f. Political riots
    g. Terrorism
    h. Political persecution and torture
    i. Extreme patriotism
    j. Extreme nationalism
    k. Constant international bickering
    l. Sabotaging of attempts at world collaboration and cooperation

14. Economic Irrationalities
    a. Ecological waste and pollution
    b. Poor use and development of natural resources
    c. Economic boycotts and wars
    d. Needless employer-employee bickering and strikes
    e. Extreme profiteering
    f. Business bribery, corruption, and theft
    g. Extreme economic status-seeking
    h. Union bribery, corruption, and graft
    i. Misleading and false advertising
    j. Foolish restrictions on business and labor
    k. Inefficiency in business and industry
    l. Addiction to foolish economic customs
    m. Inequitable and ineffectual taxes
    n. Gambling abuses
    o. Foolish consumerism (e.g, expensive funerals, dog funerals, weddings, alcohol consumption, etc.)
    p. Production of shoddy materials

     q. Lack of intelligent consumerism information and control
     r. Inefficiently run welfare systems
     s. Inefficiently run government agencies
15. Avoidance Irrationalities
     a. Procrastination
     b. Complete avoidance of important things; inertia
     c. Refusal to face important realities
     d. Oversleeping and avoidance of sufficient sleep
     e. Refusal to get sufficient exercise
     f. Lack of thought and preparation for the future
     g. Needless suicide
16. Dependency Irrationalities
     a. Need for approval and love of others
     b. Need for authority figures to run one's life
     c. Need for superhuman gods and devils
     d. Need for parents when one has matured chronologically
     e. Need for a helper, guru, or therapist
     f. Need for a hero
     g. Need for magical solutions to problems
17. Hostility Irrationalities
     a. Condemning people totally because some of their acts appear undesirable or unfair
     b. Demanding that people absolutely must do what one would like them to do and damning them when they don't
     c. Setting up perfectionistic standards and insisting that people have to follow them
     d. Commanding that justice and fairness must exist in the universe and making oneself quite incensed when they do not
     e. Insisting that hassles and difficulties must not exist and that life turns absolutely awful when they do
     f. Disliking unfortunate conditions and not merely working to overcome or remove them, but over-rebelliously hating the entire system that produced them and the people involved in this system

g. Remembering past injustices and vindictively feuding against the perpetrators of these injustices forever

h. Remembering past injustices in gory detail and obsessing about them and their perpetrators forever

18. Excitement-Seeking Irrationalities

a. Continuing to gamble compulsively in spite of serious losses

b. Leading a carousing, playboy or playgirl type of life at the expense of other, more solid enjoyments

c. Engaging in dangerous sports or pastimes, such as mountain climbing, hunting, or skiing under hazardous conditions

d. Deliberately having sex without taking contraceptive or venereal disease precautions

e. Engaging in college hazing or other pranks of a hazardous nature

f. Turning in false fire alarms

g. Dangerous forms of dueling

h. Engaging in stealing or homicide for excitement-seeking

i. Engaging in serious forms of brawling, fighting, rioting, or warring for excitement-seeking

j. Engaging in cruel sports, such as clubbing baby seals or cock-fighting for excitement-seeking

19. Magic-Related Irrationalities

a. Devout belief in magic, sorcery, witchcraft, etc.

b. Devout belief in astrology

c. Devout belief in phrenology

d. Devout belief in mediums and ghosts

e. Devout belief in talking horses and other talking animals

f. Devout belief in extrasensory perception

g. Devout belief in demons and exorcism

h. Devout belief in the power of prayer

i. Devout belief in superhuman entities and gods

j. Devout belief in damnation and salvation

k. Devout belief that the universe really cares for humans

    l. Devout belief that some force in the universe spies on humans and regulates their lives on the principle of deservingness and nondeservingness

    m. Devout belief in the unity and union of all things in the world

    n. Devout belief in immortality

20. Immorality Irrationalities

    a. Engaging in immoral and criminal acts opposed to one's own strong moral code

    b. Engaging in immoral and criminal acts for which one has a good chance of getting apprehended and severely penalized

    c. Engaging in immoral and criminal acts when one would have a good chance of gaining more with less effort at noncriminal pursuits

    d. Firmly believing that virtually no chance exists of one's getting caught at immoral and criminal acts when a good chance actually exists

    e. Strong belief that because a good chance exists that one can get away with a single criminal act, a good chance also exists that one can get away with repeated acts of that nature

    f. Stubborn refusal to amend one's immoral ways even though one suffers severe penalties for engaging in them

    g. Engaging in criminal, assaultive, or homicidal acts without any real sense of behaving irresponsibly or immorally

21. Irrationalities Related to Low Frustration Tolerance or Short-Range Hedonism

    a. Strong insistence on going mainly or only for the pleasures of the moment instead of for those of the present and future

    b. Obsession with immediate gratifications, whatever the costs

    c. Whining and strongly pitying oneself when one finds it necessary to surrender short-range pleasures for other gains

    d. Ignoring the dangers inherent in going for immediate pleasures

    e. Striving for ease and comfort rather than for greater satisfactions that require some temporary discomfort

    f. Refusing to work against a harmful addiction because of the immediate discomfort of giving it up

    g. Refusing to continue with a beneficial or satisfying program of activity because one views its onerous aspects as too hard and devoutly believes that they should not exist

    h. Chomping at the bit impatiently when one has to wait for or work for a satisfying condition to occur

    i. Procrastinating about doing activities that one knows would turn out beneficially and that one has promised oneself to do

    j. Significantly contributing to the consumption of a scarce commodity that one knows one will very much want in the future

22. Defensive Irrationalities

    a. Rationalizing about one's poor behavior instead of trying to honestly admit it and correct it

    b. Denying that one has behaved poorly or stupidly when one clearly has

    c. Avoiding facing some of one's serious problems and sweeping them under the rug

    d. Unconsciously repressing some of one's "shameful" acts because one will savagely condemn oneself if one consciously admits them

    e. Projecting one's poor behavior onto others and contending that they did it in order to deny responsibility for it

    f. Using the sour grapes mechanism, and claiming that you really do not want something you do want, when you find it too difficult to face your not getting it

    g. Identifying with outstanding individuals and unrealistically believing that you have the same kinds of abilities or talents that they have

    h. Resorting to transference: confusing people who affected you seriously in your past life with those whom you have interests in today and assuming that the present individuals will act pretty much the same way as the past ones did

    i. Resorting to a reaction formation: expressing reverse feelings (such as love) for someone for whom you really have the opposite feelings (such as hate)

23. Attribution Irrationalities

    a. Attributing to people feelings for you that they really do not have

    b. Attributing certain motives for people's behavior when they do not actually have those motives

    c. Attributing to people a special interest in you when they have no such interest

    d. Attributing certain characteristics or ideas to people because they have membership in a group whose constituents frequently have such characteristics or ideas

24. Memory-Related Irrationalities

    a. Forgetting painful experiences soon after they end and not using them to avoid future pain

    b. Embellishing the facts about people's behavior and inventing exaggerations and rumors about them

    c. Focusing mainly or only on the immediate advantages or disadvantages of things and shortsightedly ignoring what will probably happen in connection with them in the future

    d. Repressing one's memory of important events so as not to feel responsibility or shame about their occurring

    e. Remembering some things too well and thereby interfering with effective thought and behavior in other respects

25. Demandingness-Related Irrationalities

    a. Demanding that one must do well at certain goals in order to accept oneself as a human being

    b. Demanding that one must win the approval or love of significant others

    c. Demanding that one must do perfectly well at practically everything and/or win the perfect approval of practically everyone

    d. Demanding that others must treat one fairly, justly, considerately, and lovingly

    e. Demanding that everyone must treat one perfectly fairly, justly, considerately, and lovingly

    f. Demanding that the conditions of life must remain easy and that one must get practically everything one wants quickly, without any undue effort

    g. Demanding that one must have almost perfect enjoyment or ecstasy at all times

26. Sex-Related Irrationalities

    a. The belief that sex acts have intrinsic dirtiness, badness, or wickedness

    b. The belief that sex acts prove absolutely bad or immoral unless they go with love, marriage, or other nonsexual relationships

    c. The belief that orgasm has a sacred quality and that sex without it has no real joy or legitimacy

    d. The belief that intercourse has a sacred quality and that orgasm must come about during penile-vaginal intromission

    e. The belief that one must have sex competence and that one's worth as a person doesn't exist without it

    f. The belief that good sex always must include simultaneous orgasm

    g. The belief that masturbation and petting to orgasm have a shameful quality, not the legitimacy of intercourse

    h. The belief that men can legitimately and morally have more sex or less restricted sex than can women

    i. The belief that sex competence should occur spontaneously and easily, without any kind of knowledge or practice

    j. The belief that women have little natural interest in sex, remain naturally passive, and have inferior sexual abilities and capacities

  k. The belief that two people who love each other can have little or no sexual interest in other individuals

27. Science-Related Irrationalities

  a. The belief that science provides a panacea for the solution of all human problems

  b. The belief that the specific method constitutes the only method of advancing human knowledge

  c. The belief that all technological inventions and advances prove good for humans

  d. The belief that because the logico-empirical method of science does not give perfect solutions to all problems and has its limitations, it has little or no usefulness

  e. The belief that because indeterminacy exists in scientific observation, the logico-empirical method has no validity

  f. The belief that because science has found evidence and explanations for hypotheses that originally only existed in the human imagination (e.g., the theory of relativity), it has to and undoubtedly will find evidence and explanations for other imagined hypotheses (such as the existence of a soul or of God)

  g. The belief that because a scientist gets recognized as an authority in one area (e.g., Einstein as a physicist), he or she must have authoritative views in other areas (e.g., politics)

  h. The strong tendency of highly competent, exceptionally well-trained scientists to act in a highly prejudiced, foolish manner in some important aspects of their scientific endeavors, and to behave even more foolishly in their personal lives

  i. The strong tendency of applied social scientists—such as clinical psychologists, psychiatrists, social workers, counselors, and clergymen—to behave self-defeatingly and unscientifically in their personal and professional lives.

The forgoing list of human irrationalities, which in no way pretends to exhaust the field, includes 259 major happiness-sabotaging tendencies. Some of these, admittedly, overlap, so that the list includes repetitions. At the same time, it consists of only a bare outline; under each of its headings we can easily subsume a large number of other irrationalities. Under heading 1.h., for example—irrationalities related to courtship, marriage, and wedding customs—we could easily include hundreds of idiocies, many of them historical, but many still extant.

Psychotherapy represents one of the most tragic examples in this respect. It is mentioned briefly, under heading 27.i.—science-related irrationalities—as "the strong tendency of applied social scientists—such as clinical psychologists, psychiatrists, social workers, counselors, and clergymen—to behave self-defeatingly and unscientifically in their personal and professional lives." This hardly tells the tale! For psychotherapy supposedly consists of a field of scientific inquiry and application whose practitioners remain strongly devoted to helping their clients eliminate or minimize their irrational, self-destructive thoughts, feelings, and behaviors. Actually, the opposite largely appears to hold true. For most therapists seem to have almost innumerable irrational ideas and to engage in ubiquitous antiscientific activities that help their clients maintain or even intensify their unreasonableness.

A few major irrationalities of psychotherapeutic "helpers" include:

1. Instead of taking a comprehensive, multimodal, cognitive-emotive-behavioral approach to treatment, they fetishistically and obsessively-compulsively overemphasize some monolithic approach, such as awareness, insight, emotional release, understanding of the past, experiencing, rationality, or physical release.
2. They have their own dire needs for their clients' approval and frequently tie these clients to them in an extended dependency relationship.

3. They abjure scientific, empirically based analysis for far-fetched conjectures that they rarely relate to factual data.

4. They tend to focus on helping clients feel better rather than get better by learning specifically how they upset themselves and how they can stop doing so in the future.

5. They dogmatically assume that their own system or technique of therapy, and it alone, helps people, and they have a closed mind to other systems or techniques.

6. They promulgate therapeutic orthodoxies and excoriate and excommunicate deviates from their dogmas.

7. They confuse correlation with cause and effect and assume that if an individual hates, say, his mother, and later hates other women, his former feeling must have caused the latter feeling.

8. They mainly ignore the biological bases of human behavior and assume that *special* situational reasons for all disturbances must exist, and, worse yet, that if one finds these special reasons the disturbances will almost automatically disappear.

9. They tend to look for (and "find"!) unique, clever, and "deep" explanations of behavior and ignore many obvious, "superficial," and truer explanations.

10. They either promulgate the need, on the part of their clients, for interminable therapy, or they promulgate the myth that easy, quick, miracle cures exist.

11. They turn more and more to magic, faith healing, astrology, tarot cards, and other unscientific means of "transpersonal" psychotherapy.

12. They strive for vaguely defined, utopian goals that mislead and harm clients.

13. They make irrational, unscientific attacks on experimentally inclined therapists.

14. They apotheosize emotion and invent false dichotomies between reason and emotion.

This list is not exhaustive and could easily be doubled or tripled. To repeat the main point: Virtually all the main headings and sub-headings presented in the list of major human irrationalities have a score or more further subdivisions; moreover, for each subdivision a fairly massive amount of observational and experimental confirma-tory evidence exists. For example, we have a massive amount of observational evidence that innumerable people overeat, procrasti-nate, think dogmatically, lose considerable amounts of money in foolish gambling, devoutly believe in astrology, and continually ra-tionalize about their own inept behavior. In addition, we have con-siderable experimental evidence that humans feel favorably biased in regard to those whom they consider attractive, that they back-slide after giving up a habit like overeating, that they go for specious immediate gratifications instead of more enjoyable long-term satis-factions, that they repress memories of events they consider shame-ful, that they frequently attribute feelings to others that these others do not seem to have, and that they have an almost incredible degree of suggestibility in regard to an opinion of the majority of their fel-lows or of a presumed authority figure.

Granted that all the forgoing major human irrationalities—and many more like them!—exist, can one maintain the thesis that, in all probability, they have biological roots and stem from the funda-mental nature of humans? Yes, on several important, convincing grounds, which follow.

1. All the major human irrationalities seem to exist, in one form or another, in virtually all humans. Not equally, of course! On the whole, some of us behave much less irrationally than others. But go find *any* individual who does not fairly frequently subscribe to *all* of these major irrationalities. For example, using only the first ten main headings that apply to personal self-sabotaging, do you know of a single man or woman who has not often slavishly conformed to some asinine social custom; not given himself or herself global, total ratings; not held strong prejudices; not resorted to several kinds of illogical thinking; not fooled himself or herself into believing that his or her strong feelings represented something about objective re-ality; not acquired and persisted in self-defeating habits, not had

any pernicious addictions; remained perfectly free of all neurotic symptoms; never subscribed to religious dogmas; and never surrendered to any foolish health habits? Is there a single such case?

2. Just about all the major irrationalities that now exist have held rampant sway in virtually all social and cultural groups that have been investigated historically and anthropologically. Although rules, laws, mores, and standards vary widely from group to group, gullibility, absolutism, dogmas, religiosity, and demandingness *about* these standards remains surprisingly similar. Thus in the Western civilized world, your parents and your culture advise or educate you to wear one kind of clothes and, in the South Sea Islands, to wear another kind. But where they tend to inform you, "You had better dress in the right or proper way so that people will accept your behavior and act advantageously toward you," you irrationally escalate this "proper" (and not too irrational) standard into, "I *must* dress properly because I absolutely *need* other people's approval. I *can't stand* their disapproval and the disadvantages that may thereby accrue to me. And if they do not like my behavior that means they do not like *me* and that I rate as a completely *rotten person!*" Although your parents and your teachers may encourage you to think in this absolutistic, self-downing manner, you seem to have the innate human propensity (a) to gullibly take them seriously, (b) to carry on their nonsense for the rest of your life, and (c) to invent it yourself if they happen to provide you with relatively little absolutism.

3. Many of the irrationalities that people profoundly follow go counter to almost all the teachings of their parents, peers, and the mass media. Yet they refuse to give them up! Few parents encourage you to overgeneralize, make anti-empirical statements, or uphold contradictory propositions; yet you tend to do this kind of thing continually. Your educational system strongly encourages you to learn, unlearn, and relearn; yet you have great difficulty doing so in many important respects. You encounter strong persuasive efforts of others to get you to forgo nonproductive and self-defeating habits, like overeating and smoking. But you largely tend to resist this constant teaching. You may literally go, at your own choosing, for years of psychotherapy to overcome your anxiety or tendencies

toward depression. But look at the relatively little progress you often make!

You may have parents who raise you with extreme skepticism or antireligious tendencies. Yet, you easily can adopt some extreme religious orthodoxy in your adult years. You learn about the advisability of regularly visiting your physician and your dentist from grade school onward. But does this teaching make you go? Does widespread reading about the facts of life quiet your Pollyannaism or utopianism—or rid you of undue pessimism? Thousands of well-documented books and films have clearly exposed the inequities of wars, riots, terrorism, and extreme nationalism. Have they really induced you to strongly oppose these forms of political irrationality?

Virtually no one encourages you to procrastinate and to avoid facing life's realities. Dangerous excitement-seeking rarely gets you the approval of others. Does that stop you from indulging in it? The vast majority of scientists oppose magical, unverifiable, absolutistic, devout thinking. Do you always heed them? You usually know perfectly well what moral and ethical rules you subscribe to, and almost everyone you know encourages you to subscribe to them. Do you? Low frustration tolerance and short-range hedonism rarely prove acceptable to your elders, your teachers, your clergymen, and your favorite writers. Does their disapproval stop you from frequently giving in to immediate gratification at the expense of future gains? Who teaches you to rationalize and reinforces you when you do so? What therapist, friend, or parent goes along with your other kinds of defensiveness? But does their almost universal opposition stop you? Do significant others in your life reward you for demanding perfection of yourself or of them, for whining and wailing that conditions *must* transpire the way you want them to turn out?

Certainly, a good many irrationalities have an important cultural component—or at least get significantly encouraged and exacerbated by the social group. But a good many seem minimally taught, and many others get severely discouraged—yet still ubiquitously flourish!

4. As mentioned before, practically all the irrationalities listed in

this appendix hold true not only for ignorant, stupid, and severely disturbed individuals but also for highly intelligent, educated, and relatively little disturbed persons. Ph.D.s in physics and psychology, for example, have racial and other prejudices, indulge in enormous amounts of wishful thinking, believe that if someone believes something strongly—or intensely experiences it—it must have objective reality and truth, fall prey to all kinds of pernicious habits (including addictions like alcoholism), foolishly get themselves into debt, devoutly think that they must have others' approval, believe in the power of prayer, and invent rumors about others, which they then strongly believe. Unusually bright and well-educated people probably hold fewer or less rigid irrationalities than average members of the populace, but they hardly have a monopoly on rational behavior!

5. So many humans hold highly irrational beliefs and participate in exceptionally self-defeating behaviors so often that we can only with great difficulty uphold the hypothesis that they entirely learn these ways of reacting. Even if we hypothesize that they largely or mainly learn how to behave so badly, the obvious question arises: Why do they allow themselves to get taken in so badly by the teachings of their culture, and if they do imbibe these during their callow youth, why don't they teach themselves how to give up these inanities later? Almost all of us learn many significant political, social, and religious values from our parents and our institutions during our childhood, but we often give them up later—after we go to college, read some hardheaded books, or befriend people who subscribe to quite different values. Why don't we do this about many of our most idiotic and impractical views, which clearly do not accord with reality and which obviously do us considerable harm?

Take, for instance, the following ideas, which just a little reflection will show have little sense and which will almost always lead to bad results: (a) "If my sister did me in as a child, all women appear dangerous and I'd better not relate to them intimately." (b) "If I lack competency in an area, such as academic performance, I rate as a totally worthless individual and deserve no happiness." (c) "Because you have treated me unfairly, as you absolutely must not, you have to change your ways and treat me better in the future." (d) "Since I enjoy smoking very much, I can't give it up; and although others acquire serious disadvantages from continuing it, I can most probably get away with smoking without harming myself." (e) "Because blacks get arrested and convicted for more crimes than whites, they all rate as an immoral race and I'd better have nothing to do with them." (f) "If biological and hereditary factors play an important part in emotional disturbance, we can do nothing to help disturbed people, and their plight remains hopeless."

All these irrational statements, and hundreds of similar ones, clearly make little or no sense and wreak immense social and individual harm. Yet we devoutly believe them in millions of cases. Even if we can show that some significant part of these beliefs stems from social learning (as it probably does), why do we strongly imbibe and so persistently hang on to them? Clearly because we have a powerful biological predisposition to do so.

6. When bright and generally competent people give up many of their irrationalities, they frequently tend to adopt other inanities or to go to opposite irrational extremes. Devout religionists often turn into devout atheists. Political right-wing extremists wind up as left-wing extremists. Individuals who procrastinate mightily may later emerge as compulsive workers. People who surrender one irrational phobia frequently turn up with another equally irrational but quite different phobia. Extremism tends to remain as a natural human trait that takes one foolish form or another.

7. Human beings who seem least afflicted by irrational thoughts and behaviors still revert to them, and sometimes seriously so, at certain times. A man who rarely gets angry at others may on occasion incense himself so thoroughly that he almost or actually murders someone. A woman who fearlessly studies difficult subjects and takes complicated exams may feel that she can't bear rejection by a job interview and may fail to look for a suitable position. A therapist who objectively and dispassionately teaches his or her clients how to behave more rationally may, if one of them stubbornly resists, act quite irrationally and agitatedly dismiss that person from therapy. In cases like these, unusual environmental conditions often bring

out silly behavior by normally sane individuals. But these individuals obviously react to these conditions because they have some basic disposition to go out of their heads under unusual kinds of stress—and that basic disposition probably has innate elements.

8. People highly opposed to various kinds of irrationalities often fall prey to them. Agnostics give in to devout, absolutistic thoughts and feelings. Highly religious individuals act quite immorally. Psychologists who believe that guilt or self-downing has no legitimacy make themselves guilty and self-downing.

9. Knowledge or insight into one's irrational behavior only partially, if at all, helps one change it. You may know full well about the harmfulness of smoking—and smoke more than ever! You may realize that you hate sex because your parents puritanically taught you to do so, but you may nonetheless keep hating it. You may have clear-cut "intellectual" insight into your overweening egotism but have little "emotional" insight into how to change it. This largely arises from the basic human tendency to have two contradictory beliefs at the same time—an "intellectual" one you lightly and occasionally hold and an "emotional" one you vigorously and consistently hold, and which you therefore usually tend to act upon. This tendency to have simultaneous contradictory beliefs again seems part of the human condition.

10. No matter how hard and how long people work to overcome their irrational thoughts and behaviors, they usually find it exceptionally difficult to overcome or eradicate them, and to some degree they always remain exceptionally fallible in this respect. We could hypothesize that because they overlearn their self-defeating behaviors at an early age, they therefore find it most difficult to recondition themselves. But it seems simpler and more logical to conclude that their fallibility has an inherent source—and that their early conditionability and proneness to accepting training in dysfunctional behavior *itself* represents a significant part of their innate fallibility! Certainly, they hardly acquired conditionability solely through having someone condition them!

11. It appears reasonably clear that certain irrational ideas stem from personal, nonlearned (or even anti-learned) experiences, and

that we inventively, though crazily, *invent* them in a highly creative manner. Suppose, for instance, you fall in love with someone and you intensely feel, "know," and state, "I know I'll love you forever!" You certainly didn't *learn* that knowledge—since you not only read about Romeo and Juliet but also read lots of other information, such as divorce statistics, which show that people rarely romantically adore each other forever. You consequently *choose* your "knowledge" out of several other realms of data you could have chosen to "know." And you most probably did so because romantic love among humans frequently carries with it the intrinsic illusion that "Because my feeling for you has such authenticity and intensity, I *know* it will last forever." You, at least for the most part, autistically *create* the false and irrational "knowledge" that goes with your genuine (and most probably temporary) feelings.

Again, you may have been reared as a Jew or a Muslim, then convert yourself to Christianity and conclude, "I feel Jesus as my Savior, and I feel certain that He exists as the Son of God." Did your experience or your environmental upbringing lead to this feeling and belief? Or did you, for various reasons, invent it? The natural tendency of individuals seems to consist of frequent dogmatic beliefs that their profound feelings prove something objectively exists in the universe, and this largely appears an innately based process of illusion.

12. If we look closely at some of the most popular irrational forms of thinking, it appears that humans figure them out. They start with a sensible or realistic observation and end up with a non sequitur type of conclusion. Thus, you start with, "It would feel enjoyable and I would have advantages if Jane loved me." You then falsely conclude, "Therefore she *has* to love me, and I find it *awful* if she doesn't." If you begin with the even stronger observation, "It would be *exceptionally* and *uniquely enjoyable if Jane loved me*," you have even more of a tendency to conclude, "*Therefore she must!*" But no matter how true the first part of your proposition proves, the second part remains a non sequitur, making no sense whatever.

Similarly, you tend to irrationally conclude, "Because I find order desirable, I *need* certainty." "Because I find failure most undesirable,

(a) I *must* not fail, (b) I did not cause myself to fail—he made me do it, and (c) maybe I didn't really fail at all." "Because it would prove very hard for me to give up smoking, I find it *too* hard, and I *can't* do it." All these non sequiturs stem from autistic, grandiose thinking— you simply *command* that what you desire must exist and what you find obnoxious must not. This kind of autistic thinking largely appears innate.

13. Many types of irrational thinking largely consist of arrant overgeneralizations, and as Alfred Korzybski and his followers have shown, overgeneralizations seem a normal (though foolish) part of the human condition. Thus, you easily begin with a sensible observation, again: "I failed at that test," and then you overgeneralize to, "I will always fail; I have no ability to succeed at it." Or you start with, "They sometimes treat me unjustly," and you overgeneralize to, "They always treat me unjustly, and I can't stand their continual unfair treatment!" Again: this seems the way that normal individuals naturally think. Children, as J. Piaget has shown, lack good judgment until the age of seven or eight. Adults frequently lack it forever!

14. Human thinking not only significantly varies in relation to people's intelligence levels, but some forms of thinking stem largely from left-brain or right-brain functioning. Both intelligence and left-brain and right-brain functioning have a significant hereditary element and do not arise merely out of learned experiences.

15. Some forms of irrationality, such as low frustration tolerance or the seeking of the specious rewards of immediate rather than long-term gratification, exist in many lower animals as well as in humans. G. Ainslie reviews the literature on specious reward and shows how a decline in the effectiveness of rewards occurs in both animals and humans as the rewards get delayed from the time of choice. Again, a fairly clear-cut physiological and hereditary element seems obvious here.

16. Some evidence exists that people often find it much easier to learn self-defeating than nondefeating behavior. Thus, they very easily overeat but have great trouble sticking to a sensible diet. They can learn, usually from their foolish peers, to smoke ciga-

rettes, but if other peers or elders try to teach them to give up smoking or to act with more self-discipline in other ways, they resist this teaching to a fare-thee-well! They fairly easily pick up prejudices against blacks, Jews, Catholics, and Asians, but they rarely heed the teachings of thoroughly tolerant leaders. They quickly condition themselves to feel anxious, depressed, hating, and self-downing, but they take an enormous amount of time and effort getting rid of these disturbed feelings. They don't seem exactly doomed to a lifetime of stupid, foolish, asinine behavior. But pretty nearly!

Conclusion

If we define irrationality as thought, emotion, or behavior that leads to self-defeating or self-destructive consequences or that significantly interferes with the survival and happiness of the organism, we find that literally hundreds of major irrationalities exist in all societies and in virtually all humans in those societies. These irrationalities persist despite peoples' conscious determination to change: (a) Many of them oppose almost all the teachings of the individuals who follow them; they persist among highly intelligent, educated, and relatively little disturbed persons. (b) When people give them up, they usually replace them with other, sometimes just as extreme—though opposite—irrationalities. (c) People who strongly oppose them in principle nonetheless perpetuate them in practice; sharp insight into them or their origins hardly removes them. (d) Many of them appear to stem from autistic invention; they often seem to flow from deepseated and almost ineradicable human tendencies toward fallibility, overgeneralization, wishful thinking, gullibility, prejudice, and short-range hedonism. (e) They appear at least in part tied up with physiological, hereditary, and constitutional processes.

Although we can as yet make no certain or unqualified claim for the biological basis of human irrationality, such a claim now has enough evidence behind it to merit serious consideration. People naturally and easily act rationally and self-fulfillingly. Else they probably would not survive. But they also naturally and easily act against their own best interests. To some degree, their early and later environments encourage them to learn self-destructive behaviors. But how can we not conclude that they have powerful innate tendencies to listen to and agree with antihuman and inhumane teachings and—more important—to continue devoutly to believe in and idiotically carry on many of these obviously foolish, scientifically untenable teachings?

Appendix 2: How to Maintain and Enhance Your Rational Emotive Behavior Therapy Gains

If you work at using the principles and practices of rational emotive behavior therapy (REBT), you will be able to change your self-defeating thoughts, feelings, and behaviors and to feel much better than when you started therapy. Good! But you will also, at times, fall back— and sometimes far back. No one is perfect and practically all people take one step backwards to every two or three steps forward. Why? Because that is the nature of humans: to improve, to stop improving at times, and sometimes to backslide.

How can you (imperfectly!) slow down your tendency to fall back? How can you maintain and enhance your therapy goals? Here are some methods that we have tested at the Albert Ellis Institute's clinic in New York and that many of our clients have found effective.

How to Maintain Your Improvement

1. When you improve and then fall back to old feelings of anxiety, depression, or self-downing, try to remind yourself and pinpoint exactly what thoughts, feelings, and behaviors you once changed to bring about your improvement. If you again feel depressed, think back to how you previously used REBT to make yourself undepressed. For example, you may remember that:

   a. You stopped telling yourself that you were worthless and that you couldn't ever succeed in getting what you wanted.

    b. You did well in a job or a love affair and proved to yourself that you did have some ability and that you were lovable.

    c. You forced yourself to go on interviews instead of avoiding them and thereby helped yourself overcome your anxiety about them.

       Remind yourself of past thoughts, feelings, and behaviors that you have helped yourself by changing.

2. Keep thinking, thinking, and thinking Rational Beliefs (RBs) or coping statements, such as: "It's great to succeed but I can fully accept myself as a person and have enjoyable experiences even when I fail!" Don't merely parrot these statements but go over them carefully many times and think them through until you really begin to believe and feel that they are correct.

3. Keep seeking for, discovering, and disputing and challenging your Irrational Beliefs (IBs) with which you are once again upsetting yourself. Take each important Irrational Belief—such as, "I have to succeed in order to be a worthwhile person!"—and keep asking yourself: "Why is this belief true?" "Where is the evidence that my worth to myself, and my enjoyment of living, utterly depends on my succeeding at something?" "How does failing at an important task make me totally unacceptable as a human?"

      Keep forcefully and persistently disputing your Irrational Beliefs whenever you see that you are letting them creep back again. And even when you don't actively hold them, realize that they may arise once more, bring them to your consciousness, and preventively—and vigorously!—dispute them.

4. Keep risking and doing things that you irrationally fear—such as riding in elevators, socializing, job hunting, or creative writing. Once you have partly overcome one of your irrational fears, keep acting against it on a regular basis. If you feel uncomfortable in forcing yourself to do things that you are unrealistically afraid of doing, don't allow yourself to avoid doing them—or else you'll preserve your discomfort forever! Practice making yourself as *un*comfortable as you can be, in

order to eradicate your irrational fears and to become unanxious and comfortable later.

5. Try to clearly see the real difference between *healthy* negative feelings—such as those of sorrow, regret, and frustration, when you do not get some of the important things you want—and *unhealthy* negative feelings, such as depression, anxiety, self-hatred, and self-pity.

   Whenever you feel *over*concerned (panicked) or *unduly* miserable (depressed) acknowledge that you are having a statistically normal but a psychologically unhealthy feeling and that you are mainly bringing it on yourself with some dogmatic *should, ought,* or *must.*

   Realize that you are capable of changing your unhealthy (or *must*urbatory) feelings back into healthy (or preferential) ones. Take your depressed feelings and work on them until you only feel sorry and regretful. Take your anxious feelings and work on them until you only feel concerned and vigilant. Use rational emotive imagery to vividly imagine unpleasant Activating Events even before they happen; let yourself feel unhealthily upset (anxious, depressed, enraged, or self-downing) as you imagine them; then work on your feelings to change them to healthy negative emotions (concern, sorrow, annoyance, or regret) as you keep imagining some of the worst things happening. Don't give up until you actually do change your feelings.

6. Avoid self-defeating procrastination. Do unpleasant tasks fast—today! If you still procrastinate, reward yourself with certain things that you enjoy—for example, eating, vacationing, reading, and socializing—only *after* you have performed the tasks that you easily avoid. If this won't work, give yourself a severe penalty—such as talking to a boring person for two hours or burning a hundred dollar bill—every time you procrastinate.

7. Show yourself that it is an absorbing *challenge* and something of an *adventure* to maintain your emotional health and to keep yourself reasonably happy no matter what kind of misfortunes assail you. Make the uprooting of your misery one of the most important things in your life—something you are utterly de-

termined to steadily work at achieving. Fully acknowledge that you almost always have some choice about how to think, feel, and behave; then throw yourself actively into making that choice for yourself.

8. Remember—and use—the three main insights of REBT that were first outlined in *Reason and Emotion in Psychotherapy* in 1962:

    Insight No. 1: You largely *choose* to disturb yourself about the unpleasant events of your life, although you may be encouraged to do so by external happenings and by social learning. You mainly *feel the way you think*. When obnoxious and frustrating things happen to you at point A (Activating Events or Adversities), you consciously or unconsciously *select* Rational Beliefs (RBs) that lead you to feel sad and regretful and you also *select* Irrational Beliefs (IBs) that lead you to feel anxious, depressed, and self-hating.

    Insight No. 2: No matter how or when you acquired your Irrational Beliefs and your self-sabotaging habits, you now, in the present, *choose* to maintain them—and that is why you are *now* disturbed. Your past history and your present life conditions importantly *affect* you; but they don't *disturb* you. Your present *philosophy* is the main contributor to your *current* disturbance.

    Insight No. 3: There is no magical way for you to change your personality and your strong tendencies to needlessly upset yourself. Basic personality change requires persistent *work and practice*—yes, *work and practice*—to enable you to alter your Irrational Beliefs, your unhealthy feelings, and your self-destructive behaviors.

9. Steadily and unfrantically look for personal pleasures and enjoyments—such as reading, entertainment, sports, hobbies, art, science, and other vital absorbing interests. Make your major life goal not only the achievement of emotional health but also that of real enjoyment. Try to become involved in a long-term purpose, goal, or interest in which you can remain truly absorbed. A good happy life will give you something to

live for; will distract you from many serious woes; and will encourage you to preserve and to improve your mental health.

10. Try to keep in touch with several other people who know something about REBT and who can help you review some of its aspects. Tell them about problems that you have difficulty coping with and let them know how you are using REBT to overcome these problems. See if they agree with your solutions and can suggest additional and better kinds of REBT disputing that you can use to work against your Irrational Beliefs.

11. Practice using REBT with some of your friends, relatives, and associates who are willing to let you try to help them with it. The more often you use it with others, and are able to see what their IBs are and to try to talk them out of these self-defeating ideas, the more you will be able to understand the main principles of REBT and to use them with yourself. When you see other people act irrationally and in a disturbed manner, try to figure out—with or without talking to them about it—what their main Irrational Beliefs probably are and how these could be actively and vigorously disputed.

12. When you are in REBT individual or group therapy, try to tape record many of your sessions and listen to these carefully between sessions, so that some of the ideas that you learned in therapy sink in. After therapy has ended, play these tape recordings back to yourself from time to time to remind you how to deal with some of your old problems or new ones that may arise.

13. Keep reading rational writings and listening to REBT audio- and video cassettes. Included in the instruction sheet you were given when you started therapy at the Institute is a list of some of the main books and cassettes giving the principles and practices of REBT. Read and listen to several of these and keep going back to them from time to time.

How to Deal With Backsliding

1. Accept your backsliding as normal—as something that happens to almost all people who at first improve emotionally and who then fall back. See it as part of your human fallibility. Don't make yourself feel ashamed when some of your old symptoms return; and don't think that you have to handle them entirely by yourself and that it is wrong or weak for you to seek some additional sessions of therapy and to talk to your friends about your renewed problems.

2. When you backslide, look at your self-defeating *behavior* as bad and unfortunate; but refuse to put *yourself* down for engaging in this behavior. Use the highly important REBT principle of refraining from rating *you*, your *self*, or your *being* but of measuring only your *acts*, *deeds*, and *traits*. You are always a *person who* acts well or badly—and never a *good person* nor a *bad person*. No matter how badly you fall back and bring on your old disturbances again, work at fully accepting yourself *with* this unfortunate or weak behavior—and then try, and keep trying, to change your behavior.

3. Go back to the ABCs of REBT and clearly see what you did to fall back to your old symptoms. At A (Activating Event or Adversity), you usually experienced some failure or rejection. At RB (Rational Belief) you probably told yourself that you didn't *like* failing and didn't *want* to be rejected. If you only stayed with these Rational Beliefs, you would merely feel sorry, regretful, disappointed, or frustrated. But if you felt disturbed, you probably then went on to some Irrational Beliefs (IBs), such as: "I *must* not fail! It's *horrible* when I do!" "I *have to* be accepted, because if I'm not that makes me an *unlovable worthless person!*" If you reverted to these IBs, you probably felt, at C (emotional Consequence) once again depressed and self-downing.

4. When you find your Irrational Beliefs by which you are once again disturbing yourself, just as you originally used Disputing

(D) to challenge and surrender them, do so again—*immediately* and *persistently*. Thus, you can ask yourself, "Why *must* I not fail? Is it really *horrible* if I do?" And you can answer: "There is no reason why I *must* not fail, though I can think of several reasons why it would be highly undesirable. It's not *horrible* if I do fail—only distinctly *inconvenient*."

You can also Dispute your other Irrational Beliefs by asking yourself, "Where is it written that I **have** to be accepted? How do I become an *unlovable, worthless person* if I am rejected?" And you can answer: "I never *have to be* accepted, though I would very much *prefer* to be. If I am rejected, that makes me, alas, a *person who* is rejected this time by this individual under these conditions, but it hardly makes me an *unlovable, worthless person* who will always be rejected by anyone for whom I really care."

5. Keep looking for, finding, and actively and vigorously Disputing your Irrational Beliefs to which you have once again relapsed and that are now making you feel anxious or depressed. Keep doing this, over and over, until you build intellectual and emotional muscle (just as you would build physical muscle by learning how to exercise and then by *continuing* to exercise).

6. Don't fool yourself into believing that if you merely change your language you will always change your thinking. If you neurotically tell yourself, "I *must* succeed and be approved" and you change this self-statement to "I *prefer* to succeed and be approved," you may still really be convinced, "But I really *have to* do well to be loved." Before you stop your Disputing and before you are satisfied with your answers to it, keep on doing it until you are *really* convinced of your rational answers and until your feelings of disturbance truly disappear. Then do the same thing many, many times—until your new E (Effective Philosophy) becomes hardened and habitual—which it almost always will if you keep working at arriving at it and thinking it through.

7. Convincing yourself lightly or "intellectually" of your new Effective Philosophy or Rational Beliefs often won't help very much or persist very long. Do so very *strongly* and *vigorously*, and do so many times. Thus, you can *powerfully* convince yourself, until you really *feel* it: "I do not *need* what I *want!* I never *have to* succeed, no matter how much I *wish* to do so!" "I *can* stand being rejected by someone I care for. It won't *kill* me—and I *still* can lead a happy life!" "No human is damnable and worthless—including and especially *me!*"

How to Generalize from Working on One Emotional Problem to Working on Other Problems

1. Show yourself that your present emotional problem and the ways in which you bring it on are not unique and that most emotional and behavioral difficulties are largely created by Irrational Beliefs (IBs). Whatever your IBs are, you can overcome them by strongly and persistently disputing and acting against them.

2. Recognize that you tend to have three major kinds of Irrational Beliefs that lead you to disturb yourself and that the emotional and behavioral problems that you want to relieve fall into one, two, or all three of these categories:

   a. "I *must* do well and *have to* be approved by people whom I find important." This IB leads you to feel anxious, depressed, and self-hating; and to avoid doing things at which you may fail or avoiding relationships that may not turn out well.

   b. "Other people *must* treat me fairly and nicely!" This IB contributes to your feeling angry, furious, violent, and over-rebellious.

   c. "The conditions under which I live *must* be comfortable and free from major hassles!" This IB tends to bring about feelings of low frustration tolerance and self-pity; and sometimes those of anger and depression.

3. Recognize that when you employ one of these three absolutistic *musts*—or any of the innumerable variations on it—you naturally and commonly derive from them other irrational conclusions, such as:

   a. "Because I am not doing as well as I *must*, I am an incompetent worthless individual!" (Self-downing).

   b. "Since I am not being approved by people whom I find important, as I *have to* be, it's *awful* and *terrible!*" (Awfulizing).

   c. "Because others are not treating me as fairly and as nicely as they *absolutely should* treat me, they are *utterly rotten people* and deserve to be damned!" (Damnation).

   d. "Since the conditions under which I live are not that comfortable and since my life has several major hassles, as it *must* not have, *I can't stand it!* My existence is a horror!" (Can't-stand-it-itis).

   e. "Because I have failed and gotten rejected as I absolutely *ought not* have done, I'll *always* fail and *never* get accepted as I *must* be! My life will be hopeless and joyless forever!" (Overgeneralizing).

4. Work at seeing that these Irrational Beliefs are part of your *general* repertoire of thoughts and feelings and that you bring them to many different kinds of situations. Realize that in most cases where you feel seriously upset and act in a self-defeating manner you are consciously or unconsciously sneaking in one or more of these IBs. Consequently, if you reduce them in one area and are still emotionally disturbed about something else, you can use the same REBT principles to discover your IBs in the new area and to minimize them there.

5. Repeatedly show yourself that you normally won't disturb yourself and remain disturbed if you abandon your absolutistic *shoulds*, *oughts*, and *musts* and consistently replace them with flexible and unrigid (though still strong) *desires* and *preferences*.

6. Continue to acknowledge that you can change your Irrational Beliefs (IBs) by rigorously (not rigidly!) using realistic and healthy thinking. You can show yourself that your Irrational

Beliefs are only assumption or hypotheses—not facts. You can logically, realistically, and pragmatically Dispute them in many ways such as these:

a. You can show yourself that your IBs are self-defeating—that they interfere with your goals and your happiness. For if you firmly convince yourself, "I *must* succeed at important tasks and *have to* be approved by all the significant people in my life," you will of course at times fail and be disapproved—and thereby inevitably make yourself anxious and depressed instead of sorry and frustrated.

b. Your Irrational Beliefs do not conform to reality—and especially do not conform to the facts of human fallibility. If you always *had to* succeed, if the universe commanded that you *must* do so, you obviously *would* always succeed. But of course you often don't! If you invariably *had to* be approved by others, you could never be disapproved. But obviously you frequently are! The universe is clearly not arranged so that you will always get what you demand. So although your desires are often realistic, your godlike commands definitely are not.

c. Your Irrational Beliefs are illogical, inconsistent, or contradictory. No matter how much you *want* to succeed and to be approved, it never follows that therefore you *must* do well in these (or any other) respects. No matter how desirable justice or politeness is, it never *has to* exist.

   Although REBT disputing is not infallible or sacred, it efficiently helps you to discover which of your beliefs are irrational and self-defeating and how to use realistic, pragmatic, and logical thinking to minimize them. If you keep using flexible thinking, you will avoid dogma and set up your assumptions about you, other people, and world conditions so that you always keep them open to change.

7. Try to set up some main goals and purposes in life—goals that you would like very much to reach but that you never tell yourself that you absolutely *must* attain. Keep checking to see

how you are coming along with these goals, and at times revise them. Keep yourself oriented toward the goals that you select and that are not harmful to you or to others. Instead of making yourself extremely self-interested or socially interested, a balanced absorption in both these kinds of goals will often work out best for you and the community in which you choose to live.

8. If you get bogged down and begin to lead a life that seems too miserable or dull, review the points made in this pamphlet and work at using them. If you fall back or fail to go forward at the pace you prefer, don't hesitate to return to therapy for some booster sessions or to join one of the Institute's regular therapy groups.

Appendix 3: Techniques for Disputing Irrational Beliefs (DIBS)

If you want to increase your rationality and reduce your self-defeating irrational beliefs, you can spend at least ten minutes every day asking yourself the following questions and carefully thinking through (not merely parroting!) the healthy answers. Write down each question and your answers to it on a piece of paper; or else record the questions and your answers on a tape recorder.

1. *What self-defeating irrational belief do I want to dispute and surrender?*
   - *Illustrative Answer:* I must receive love from someone for whom I really care.
2. *Can I rationally support this belief?*
   - *Illustrative Answer:* No.
3. *What evidence exists of the falseness of this belief?*
   - *Illustrative Answer:* Many indications exist that the belief that I must receive love from someone for whom I really care is false:
   a. No law of the universe exists that says that someone I care for must love me (although I would find it nice if that person did!).
   b. If I do not receive love from one person, I can still get it from others and find happiness that way.
   c. If no one I care for ever cares for me, which is very unlikely, I can still find enjoyment in friendships, in work, in books, and in other things.
   d. If someone I deeply care for rejects me, that will be most unfortunate; but I will hardly die!

   e. Even though I have not had much luck in winning great love in the past, that hardly proves that I must gain it now.

   f. No evidence exists for any absolutistic must. Consequently, no proof exists that I must always have anything, including love.

   g. Many people exist in the world who never get the kind of love they crave and who still lead happy lives.

   h. At times during my life I know that I have remained unloved and happy; so I most probably can feel happy again under unloving conditions.

   i. If I get rejected by someone for whom I truly care, that may mean that I possess some poor, unlovable traits. But that hardly means that I am a rotten, worthless, totally un-lovable individual.

   j. Even if I had such poor traits that no one could ever love me, I would still not have to down myself as a lowly, bad individual.

4. ***Does any evidence exist of the truth of this belief?***

   • *Illustrative Answer:* No, not really. Considerable evidence exists that if I love someone dearly and never am loved in return that I will then find myself disadvantaged, inconvenienced, frustrated, and deprived. I certainly would prefer, therefore, not to get rejected. But no amount of inconvenience amounts to a horror. I can still stand frustration and loneliness. They hardly make the world awful. Nor does rejection make me a turd! Clearly, then, no evidence exists that I must receive love from someone for whom I really care.

5. ***What are the worst things that could actually happen to me if I don't get what I think I must (or do get what I think I must not get)?***

   • *Illustrative Answer:* If I don't get the love I think I must receive:

   a. I would get deprived of various possible pleasures and conveniences.

   b. I would feel inconvenienced by having to keep looking for love elsewhere.

   c. I might never gain the love I want, and thereby continue indefinitely to feel deprived and disadvantaged.

d. Other people might down me and consider me pretty worthless for getting rejected—and that would be annoying and unpleasant.

e. I might settle for pleasures other than and worse than those I could receive in a good love relationship; and I would find that distinctly undesirable.

f. I might remain alone much of the time; which again would be unpleasant.

g. Various other kinds of misfortunes and deprivations might occur in my life—none of which I need define as awful, terrible, or unbearable.

6. ***What good things could I make happen if I don't get what I think I must (or do get what I think I must not get)?***

a. If the person I truly care for does not return my love, I could devote more time and energy to winning someone else's love—and probably find someone better for me.

b. I could devote myself to other enjoyable pursuits that have little to do with loving or relating, such as work or artistic endeavors.

c. I could find it challenging and enjoy-able to teach myself to live happily without love.

d. I could work at achieving a philosophy of fully accepting myself even when I do not get the love I crave.

You can take any one of your major irrational beliefs—your *shoulds*, *oughts*, or *musts*—and spend at least ten minutes every day, often for a period of several weeks, actively and vigorously disputing this belief. To help keep yourself devoting this amount of time to the DIBS method of rational disputing, you may use operant conditioning or self-management methods (originated by B. F. Skinner, David Premack, Marvin Goldfried, and other psychologists). Select some activity that you highly enjoy that you tend to do every day—such as reading, eating, television viewing, exercising, or social contact with friends. Use this activity as a reinforcer or reward by *only* allowing yourself to engage in it *after* you have practiced Disputing Irrational Beliefs (DIBS) for at least ten minutes that day. Otherwise, no reward!

In addition, you may penalize yourself every single day you do not use DIBS for at least ten minutes. How? By making yourself perform some activity you find distinctly unpleasant—such as eating something obnoxious, contributing to a cause you hate, getting up a half-hour earlier in the morning, or spending an hour conversing with someone you find boring. You can also arrange with some person or group to monitor you and help you actually carry out the penalties and lack of rewards you set for yourself. You may of course steadily use DIBS without any self-reinforcement, since it becomes reinforcing in its own right after awhile. But you may find it more effective at times if you use it along with rewards and penalties that you execute immediately after you practice or avoid practicing this ratio-nal emotive behavior method.

Summary of Questions to Ask Yourself in DIBS

1. *What self-defeating irrational belief do I want to dispute and surrender?*
2. *Can I rationally support this belief?*
3. *What evidence exists of the falseness of this belief?*
4. *Does any evidence exist of the truth of this belief?*
5. *What are the worst things that could actually happen to me if I don't get what I think I must (or do get what I think I must not get)?*
6. *What good things could I make happen if I don't get what I think I must (or do get what I think I must not get)?*

Disputing (D) your dysfunctional or irrational Beliefs (iBs) is one of the most effective of REBT techniques. But it is still often ineffective, because you can easily and very strongly hold on to an iB (such as, "I absolutely must be loved by so-and-so, and it's awful and I am an inadequate person when he/she does not love me!"). When you question and challenge this iB you often can come up with an

Effective New Philosophy (E) that is accurate but weak: "I guess that there is no reason why so-and-so must love me, because there are other people who will love me when so-and-so does not. I can there-fore be reasonably happy without his/her love." Believing this almost Effective New Philosophy, and believing it lightly, you can still easily and forcefully believe, "Even though it is not awful and terrible when so-and-so does not love me, it really is! No matter what, I still need his/her affection!"

Weak, or even moderately strong, Disputing will therefore often not work very well to help you truly disbelieve some of your power-ful and long-held iBs; while vigorous, persistent Disputing is more likely to work.

One way to do highly powerful, vigorous Disputing is to use a tape recorder and to state one of your strong irrational Beliefs into it, such as, "If I fail this job interview I am about to have, that will prove that I'll never get a good job and that I might as well apply only for low-level positions!"

Figure out several Disputes to this iB and strongly present them on this same tape. For example: "Even if I do poorly on this inter-view, that will only show that I failed this time, but will never show that I'll always fail and can never do well in other interviews. Maybe they'll still hire me for the job. But if they don't, I can learn by my mistakes, can do better in other interviews, and can finally get the kind of job that I want."

Listen to your Disputing in an audio recording. Let other people, including your therapist or members of your therapy group, listen to it. Do it over in a more forceful and vigorous manner and let them listen to it again, to see if you are disputing more forcefully, until they agree that you are getting better at doing it. Keep listen-ing to it until you see that you are able to convince yourself and oth-ers that you are becoming more powerful and more convincing.

Selected References

Following are some of the main references I used in writing this book—together with some additional materials on Rational Emotive Behavior Therapy (REBT) and Cognitive Behavior Therapy (CBT) for readers who wish to use them for self-help purposes. Considerable other materials on REBT, including lectures and workshops for the public and for the mental health profession, are included in the free catalog of the Albert Ellis Institute, which is updated every six months. To receive a copy, send your mailing address to Albert Ellis Institute, 145 East 32nd Street, 9th Floor, New York, NY 10016; phone: (212) 535-0822; E-mail: info@albertellis.org.

Bandura, A. (1977). *Self-efficacy: The exercise of control*. New York: Freeman.

Beal, D., Kopec, A., & DiGiuseppe, R. (1996). *Disputing clients' irrational beliefs*. In manuscript.

Beck, A. T. (1976). *Cognitive therapy and the emotional disorders*. New York: New American Library.

Beck, J. S. (1995). *Cognitive therapy: Basics and beyond*. New York: Guilford.

Benson, H. (1975). *The relaxation response*. New York: Morrow.

Chase, S. (1964). *The tyranny of words*. New York: Harcourt Brace Jovanovich.

Cohen, E. D. (1992). *Caution: Faulty thinking can be harmful to your happiness*. Fort Pierce, FL: Trace-WilCo Publishers.

———. (2003). *What would Aristotle do?* Amherst, NY: Prometheus Books.

Dawkin, R. (1976). *The selfish gene*. New York: Oxford University Press.

DiGiuseppe, R. (1986). The implication of the philosophy of science for rational-emotive theory and therapy. *Psychotherapy, 23,* 634–639.

————, Leaf, R., & Linscott, J. (1993). The therapeutic relationship in rational-emotive therapy: A preliminary analysis. *Journal of Rational-Emotive and Cognitive-Behavior Therapy, 4,* 223–233.

————, & Muran, J. C. (1992). The use of metaphor in rational-emotive psychotherapy. *Psychotherapy in Private Practice, 10,* 151–165.

Dryden, W. (1990). *Dealing with anger problems: Rational-emotive therapeutic interventions.* Sarasota, FL: Professional Resource Exchange.

————. (1995). *Brief rational emotive behavior therapy.* London: Wiley.

————. (1998). *Developing self-acceptance.* Chichester, England: Wiley.

————, DiGiuseppe, R., & Neenan, M. (2003). *A primer on rational emotive behavior therapy.* Lafayette, IL: Research Press.

————, & Ellis, A. (2003). *Albert Ellis live.* London: Sage Publications.

————, & Gordon, J. (1991). *Think your way to happiness.* London: Sheldon Press.

————, & Neenan, M. (2003). *The rational emotive behavioral approach to therapeutic change.* London: Sage.

————, Walker, J., & Ellis, A. (1996). *REBT self-help form.* New York: Albert Ellis Institute.

Ellis, A. (1954). *The American sexual tragedy.* New York: Twayne.

————. (1958). Rational psychotherapy. *Journal of General Psychology, 59,* 35–49. Reprinted: New York: Albert Ellis Institute.

————. (1962). *Reason and emotion in psychotherapy.* Secaucus, NJ: Citadel.

————. (1975). *A garland of rational humorous songs.* New York: Albert Ellis Institute.

————. (1976). The biological basis of human irrationality. *Journal of Individual Psychology, 32,* 145–168. Reprinted: New York: Albert Ellis Institute.

———. (1984). *A guide to personal happiness.* North Hollywood, CA: Wilshire Books.

———. (1992). *Unconditionally accepting yourself and others.* Cassette recording. New York: Albert Ellis Institute.

———. (1999). *How to make yourself happy and remarkably less disturbable.* Atascadero, CA: Impact Publishers.

———. (2000a). *Feeling better, getting better, and staying better.* Atascadero, CA: Impact Publishers.

———. (2000b). *How to control your anxiety before it controls you.* New York: Citadel Press.

———. (2000c). Spiritual goals and spirited values in psychotherapy. *Journal of Individual Psychology, 56,* 277–284.

———. (2001). *Overcoming destructive beliefs, feelings, and behaviors.* Amherst, NY: Prometheus Books.

———. (2002a). *Overcoming resistance: A rational emotive behavior therapy integrative approach.* New York: Springer.

———. (2002b). Idiosyncratic REBT. In W. Dryden (Ed.), *Idiosyncratic REBT* (pp. 15–29). Russon-Wye, England: PCCB Books.

———. (2003a). *Anger: How to live with and without it.* Rev. ed. New York: Citadel Press.

———. (2003b). *Ask Albert Ellis.* Atascadero, CA: Impact Publishers.

———. (2003c) General semantics and rational emotive behavior therapy. In I. Caro & C. S. Read (Eds.), *General semantics in psychotherapy* (pp. 297–323). Brooklyn, NY: Institute for General Semantics.

———. (2004a). *Rational emotive behavior therapy: It works for me—it can work for you.* Amherst, NY: Prometheus Books.

———. (2004b). *The road to tolerance: The philosophy of rational emotive behavior therapy.* Amherst, NY: Prometheus Books.

———. (2005). Rational emotive behavior therapy. In R. J. Corsini & D. Widding (Eds.), *Current psychotherapies.* Belmont, CA: Thompson.

———, & Blau, S. (Eds.). (1998). *The Albert Ellis reader.* New York: Kensington Publishers.

Epictetus. (1890). *The works of Epictetus.* Boston: Little Brown, 1899.

Epicurus. (1996). *A guide to happiness.* London: Orion Books.

Fisher, R., Ury, W., & Patton, B. (1991). *Getting to yes.* 2nd ed. New York: Penguin Books.

Flett, G. L., & Hewitt, P. L. (2002). *Perfectionism: Theory research and training.* Washington, DC: American Psychological Association.

Frankl, V. (1960). *Man's search for meaning.* New York: Pocket Books.

Frazer, J. G. (1959). *The golden bough.* New York: Macmillan.

Freud, A. (1946). *The ego and the mechanics of defense.* London: Hogarth.

Freud, S. (1938). *Basic writings.* New York: Modern Library.

Froggatt, W. (1993). *Choose to be happy.* New Zealand: HarperCollins.

Fromm, E. (1955). *The sane society.* New York: Rinehart.

Hallowell, E. M. (1997). *Worry: Controlling it and using it wisely.* New York: Pantheon.

Hauck, P. A. (1991). *Overcoming the rating game: Beyond self-love—beyond self-esteem.* Louisville, KY: Westminster/John Knox.

Hayes, S. C., Strosahl, K., & Wilson, K. G. (1999). *Acceptance and commitment therapy.* New York: Guilford.

Hoffer, E. (1951). *The true believer.* New York: Harper & Row.

Jacobson, E. (1938). *You must relax.* New York: McGraw-Hill.

Kelly, G. (1955). *The psychology of personal constructs.* New York: Norton.

Korzybski, A. (1933/1990). *Science and sanity.* Concord, CA: International Society for General Semantics.

Leifer, R. (1997). *The happiness project.* Ithaca, NY: Snow Lion Publications.

———. (1999, March). Buddhist conceptualization and treatment of anger. *Journal of Clinical Psychology, In Session, 55,* 340–351.

Maultsby, M.C., Jr. (1971). Rational emotive imagery. *Rational Living,* 6(1), 24–27.

———. (1984). *Rational emotive therapy.* Englewood Cliffs, NJ: Prentice-Hall.

Meichenbaum, D. (1992). Evolution of cognitive behavior therapy: Origins, tenets, and clinical examples. In J. K. Zeig (Ed.), *The evo-*

lution of psychotherapy: The second conference (pp. 114–128). New York: Brunner/Mazel.

Niebuhr, R. See Pietsch, W. V.

Padesky, C. A., & Beck, A. T. (2001). Science and philosophy: Comparison of cognitive therapy and rational emotive behavior therapy. *Journal of Cognitive Therapy, 17,* 211–224.

Pavlov, I. P. (1927). *Conditional reflexes.* New York: Limelight.

Peale, N. V. (1952). *The power of positive thinking.* New York: Fawcett.

Pietsch, W. V. (1993). *The serenity prayer.* San Francisco: Harper San Francisco.

Popper, K. R. (1962). *Objective knowledge.* London: Oxford.

———. (1985). *Popper selections.* Ed. by David Miller. Princeton, NJ: Princeton University Press.

Rogers, C. (1961). *On becoming a person.* Boston: Houghton Mifflin.

Rokeach, M. (1960). *The open and closed mind.* New York: Basic Books.

Skinner, B. F. (1971). *Beyond freedom and dignity.* New York: Knopf.

Walen, S., DiGiuseppe, R., & Dryden, W. (1992). *A practitioner's guide to rational-emotive therapy.* New York: Oxford.

Watson, J. B. (1919). *Psychology from the standpoint of a behaviorist.* Philadelphia: Lippincott.

Index

About the Authors

ALBERT ELLIS, PH.D., founded Rational Emotive Behavior Therapy (REBT), the pioneering form of modern Cognitive Behavior Therapies (CBT). In a 1982 professional survey, Dr. Ellis was ranked as the second most influential psychotherapist in history. His name remains well known among psychologists, students, and historians around the world. He published over seven hundred articles and more than sixty books on psychotherapy, marital and family therapy, and sex therapy. Until his death in 2007, Dr. Ellis served as President Emeritus of the Albert Ellis Institute in New York, which provides professional training programs and psychotherapy to individuals, families and groups. To learn more, visit www.albertellis.org.

KRISTENE A. DOYLE, PH.D., SC.D. is Director of the Albert Ellis Institute. Dr. Doyle is also the director of Clinical Services, founding director of the Eating Disorders Treatment and Research Center, and a licensed psychologist at the Institute. She is a diplomate in Rational-Emotive and Cognitive-Behavior Therapy and serves on the Diplomate Board. In addition, Dr. Doyle conducts numerous workshops and professional trainings throughout the world and has influenced the growth and practice of Rational Emotive and Cognitive Behavior Therapy in countries spanning several continents. Dr. Doyle is co-author of *A Practitioner's Guide to Rational Emotive Behavior Therapy*, 3rd edition, and co-editor of *The Journal of Rational-Emotive and Cognitive-Behavior Therapy*. She has served as an expert commentator for ABC's *20/20*, *Access Hollywood*, and Channel 2 and Channel 11 News (in New York). Dr. Doyle has also been quoted in prestigious publications, including *The New York Times*, *U.S. News and World Report*, and *The Wall Street Journal*.